Pherom

Understanding th
of Sexual Attraction

D0730941

DATE DUE

DEMCO, INC. 38-3012

William Regelson M.D.

Pheromones

Understanding the Mystery of Sexual Attraction

By William Regelson M.D.

Published by:
Smart Publications™
PO Box 4667
Petaluma, CA 94955

Fax: 707 763 3944
www.smart-publications.com

First Printing 2002
Printed in the United States of America
First Edition

ISBN: 1-890572-16-0 $14.95 Softcover

Warning - Disclaimer

Smart Publications™ has designed this book to provide information in regard to the subject matter covered. It is sold with the understanding that the publisher and the author are not liable for the misconception or misuse of the information provided. Every effort has been to make this book as complete and as accurate as possible. The purpose of this book is to educate. The author and Smart Publications™ shall have neither liability nor responsibility to any person or entity with respect to any loss, damage, or injury caused or alleged to be caused directly or indirectly by the information contained in this book. The information presented herein is in no way intended as a substitute for medical counseling.

About The Author

WILLIAM REGELSON, M.D., is a Professor at the Virginia Commonwealth University College of Medicine, in Richmond. A specialist in medical oncology, with joint appointments in microbiology and biomedical engineering, he has been a leading researcher in the field of aging for more than twenty-five years. He is the former scientific director of the Fund for Integrative Biomedical Research, which was dedicated to research on the biology of aging. Dr. Regelson is also co-author of the cutting-edge, best-selling books *The Melatonin Miracle* and *The Super-Hormone Promise* related to the age decline in hormones necessary for reproductive heath and the avoidance of debility and dependency.

Table of Contents

Preface

Why do we fall in love? And why are we drawn to certain individuals and not to others? When in love, why is it that our affection often begins with kissing and later progresses to oral sex? Does our individual sexual identity spring only from social conditioning and genetic inclination? We believe all these things are influenced directly by pheromones or chemical messages that all of us are constantly exchanging with one another – with or without our conscious awareness.

We see pheromones to be part of our inheritance beyond observations in insects and rutting dogs. Our view about their place in kissing, oral sex, and homosexual and heterosexual choice was not based on controlled studies, but on the author's personal experience in dealing with the vagaries of passion, love, and limerance (joy).

We believe that odor, or chemo-attraction is a principal force in the sexual attraction and sexual identity of humans. This means that odor as a constituent of our behavior is not incidental, but essential to our continued survival and the quality of our lives.

In 1959, Butenandt was the first to identify the importance of odor as a factor in animal sexual attraction in insect physiology when he chemically isolated the odor of female moths that irresistibly attracts male moths. Karlson and Luscher (1959) named these chemical messages sexual attractants, and called them pheromones, which are species-specific chemical signals that govern behavior. There are now hundreds of such chemicals that have been clearly identified in insect, fish, amphibian, reptile, and mammalian physiology. They dramatically alter behavior in a specific fashion and are instrumental in social and sexual activity.

We feel that as knowledge about pheromones continues to grow, their clinical use will increase and result in advances in the prevention and treatment of many health concerns including aging and menopause, as well as revolutionize areas of medicine such as psychiatry. As continuing research and clinical and recreational use of pheromone-based products also increases, this will help explain why our hormones and our behavior have such profound effects on one another.

The continuing debate surrounding pheromones will only prompt further research for more uses that might greatly benefit many people. Currently, there has been an emphasis on the use of pheromone-based products to enhance social confidence and sexual attractiveness. Although we live in a socially progressive era, to detractors that might question the use of such products, it is important to widen the scope of the impact of pheromone-based products. Beyond hearing, taste, touch, and vision, the awareness of pheromones through a process separate but related to olfaction, should not upset our religious values but should reinforce them. In this book we will discuss the important role pheromones play in bonding, nurturing, and family structure, as all are influenced by our often subconscious awareness of pheromones. The emotional bonding that occurs between lovers, parent and child, and even close friends all depend on our ability to detect and respond to pheromones (body odors) that draw us together beyond our conscious control.

Many people have contributed to the publication of this book. This text owes its existence to the late David Manning White, best known as co-editor of "Mass Culture in America." The years before he died in December 1993, he and his wife, Catherine, helped to see this work finalized. During this process we have had several editors which include Alexia Dorszynski and Carol Kahn. We owe its publication to Sava Alcantara, who provided the final editing, and to John Morgenthaler, who has brought our message to the public and made possible the commercial availability of a human pheromone-based product.

> *"In copulation and it's consequences, we are mainly animals, but with our intelligence, we should seek all possible forms of pleasure in copulation and everything else."*
> — Walter – (Anonymous) "My Secret Life"

Introduction

Pheromones and the Art of Sexual Attraction

Poets, philosophers, and scientists have all tried to describe, explain, and dissect the mystery behind what attracts one person to another. What some call "chemistry" or "love at first sight," might, in fact, be more accurately described as "love at first smell." Calling attention to the universal dance that occurs between two people, recent studies have identified yet another component to the art of sexual attraction: the role of pheromones.

Pheromones are secretions produced by all healthy people and detected by a special organ inside the nose. Secreted by glands on the scalp, under the arms, and on the genitals, pheromones can be described as the silent siren call that each sex transmits to the other. We are able to detect pheromones through a special organ in the nose that allows smells and odors – especially ones we are not consciously aware of – to reach our limbic, or "primitive brain." It is here that our responses for flight or fight are triggered and it is here that we are stimulated to flirt and pursue one another.

How does this play into what attracts us to a potential lover? Once fired and detected, pheromones can result in an immediate attraction between two people. Although researchers are still figuring out exactly how it works, they do know its effect: people can become inexplicably attracted to other people. In scenes played out in airports, offices, and restaurants, it is this subtle but powerful detection of pheromones that can ignite sexual attraction between two people.

Why have we not heard more about pheromones before? Surprisingly, up until as recently as the mid-80s many in the medical community believed that the vomeronasal organ (VNO), located inside the nose, was a vestigial organ, one that had lost its functionality through the course of evolution.

Today, it is known that almost every healthy person indeed has a VNO, and it is capable of generating and detecting pheromones. What's more, this is a subconscious process that takes place instantly without our overt awareness of it. However, if two people meet and begin to "hit it off," you can be certain each is producing, transmitting, and receiving pheromones – silently but effectively.

Why is this discovery so important? Pheromones play a key role in the bonding between mother and child and between lovers. And, in stark contrast to what Freud believed, we will argue that gender identification and sexual orientation and preference is heavily influenced by pheromonal imprinting – and "determined" by one's preference for the pheromones of one sex or another. Heterosexuality and homosexuality is determined by one's preference for a particular odor or pheromone – that of a man or of a woman.

Lastly, we will show how sexual practices such as kissing and oral sex is driven by a response to pheromones produced from glands on the face and on the genitals. What begins with kissing can often lead to oral-genital contact – and we will argue that we are "hard wired" to do these things. Aside from the physical pleasure these activities provide, both also promote emotional bonding that can help build and sustain a relationship and affect our morale so important to sexual confidence.

Each of these concepts demonstrates the important role that pheromones play not only in our sexual health, but how it contributes to our sexual maturation and ability to establish healthy relationships.

Perhaps the most well-known study regarding pheromones is the study conducted in 1988 by researchers Stern and McClintock wherein college-aged women living together synchronized their menstrual cycles after a number of them were exposed to pheromones generated by others in their group. Pheromone secretions were gathered from special pads worn under the arm and later collected and swabbed on the upper lip of several women. It was learned that one woman acted as the "driver," establishing the dominant menstrual cycle that the other women followed. In later studies, a similar synchrony was established between mothers and daughters living in the same household.

As these studies and others like them demonstrate, regular exposure to pheromones from both sexes can provide health benefits. In studies conducted by Winnifred Cutler, Ph.D. as part of the Stanford Menopause Study in 1977, it was discovered that these benefits included better endocrine health, defined as healthy estrogen levels and a decreased risk for developing osteoporosis and heart disease.

To date, there are a few pheromone-based commercial products that are often described as enabling the users to boost their social confidence and as a result, enhance their existing intimate relationships, as well as improve business and other social relationships.

More studies are needed to more fully examine the potential for other therapeutic uses of pheromone-based products. For instance, menopausal women might be able to employ pheromonal-based products to help revive estrogen levels that are needed for good health. And, in the arena of the workaday world, commercial pheromone-based products might be considered particularly useful in fields that rely heavily on person-to-person contact – such as in sales and customer relations.

Whatever the application, awareness of the role that pheromones play in our sexual health and overall well-being is long overdue. Before scientists confirmed its presence, the magic of pheromones has always existed. And, with the likelihood of additional research and the future development of new products, the number of practical applications of pheromones can only continue to grow.

Most of us, at one time or another, have wondered what it is that has determined our sexual identity, choice of lovers, and even our actual sexual performance. In this book we will present what seems to us to be cogent, persuasive grounds for linking a major part of this to sexually-mediated pheromones, i.e. olfactory attractants. We will also show that the role of odor in our human interactions distinctly relates to our evolutionary past and the special features that have led to humankind's dominance of the world and the development of our social structure.

First, however, we need to understand that our sensitivity to odor, with its effects on our behavior is not something that usually enters our conscious awareness, but can be repressed, remaining hidden in our subconscious. This olfactory subconscious, while a remnant of our primitive brain, is a key to broad aspects of human behavior.

There are special anatomic features of our brain that relate responses to odor with distinct behavior. The accessory olfactory lobe distributed in our brain, which responds to sexual scent signals, triggers a wide range of behavior, influencing but isolated from cognitive control. These responses include sexual behavior such as courtship, reproductive behavior, and maternal response.

Also important to human behavior are the influence of these odors on male aggression. Thus, our interest in odor awareness must not be restricted to love and romance, but also include the origin of group hatred, madness, and war.

This book is an effort to focus scientific and public attention to pheromones, scent signals which serve communication between members of the same species. Pheromones elicit immediate behavioral responses or over time they trigger endocrine or neurophysiological responses of significance to species survival.

Pheromones, as mentioned previously, were first discovered as paramount mediators of insect behavior. But, they are also active in mammals, including our own species. These special scent signals are detected by unique nasal receptors directed to specialized brain centers that have preserved their identity throughout vertebrate evolution. Pheromones are scents, sexually derived, that are distinct from odors related to food or noxious stimuli. Specialized nasal receptors, nerves, and brain centers are required for their determination.

These special odors can be likened to a finger stretching through our nasal passages and tickling sexually essential brain areas. They impinge on anatomically distinct areas which, although interactive with the main olfactory system, are functionally different.

The study of pheromonal influences in animals cover a wide range of instinctive and/or sexually important responses. Although, until recently, humans were thought to be distinct from other mammals because of our lack of response to pheromones, Wiener, in 1966 saw their importance as critical to human normal and pathological behavior. He coined the term, "external chemical messengers" (ECMs) and provided evidence for an olfactory pheromone-influenced subconscious in humans. Wiener developed the concept that external chemical messengers (ECMs), pheromones, or as he termed them, ectohormones, could be responsible for human behavior, and, most importantly, mental illness.

Wiener's observations were ahead of their time, but he anticipated the important role for pheromones, sexual odors, in human physiology long before anyone else. It was his hypothesis, apart from the role of skin in pheromonal production, that tears, saliva, blushing, coughing, and yawning were also physiologic devices emitting pheromones. Most importantly, he anticipated that pheromonal stimuli provides a channel of nonverbal communication and that pheromones could be received as a "stimuli beyond those consciously noted" in taste and smell.

He postulated that hallucinogens, e.g., LSD, can act as stimuli to pheromonal production or sensitivity and that pheromones act as signals that may be incorporated into our unconscious thought processes. He observed that humans perceived sex odors via smell with profound effects on human sexual response.

It was Weiner's thesis that these pheromones constituted an olfactory language based on their chemical components, i.e., steroids, amines, indoles, and fatty acids, making up a vocabulary wherein emission of mixtures of these substances provide a sensory language. Rapidly changing olfactory signals provide a script of specific meaning to the recipient.

Wiener labels our response to this olfactory language, "the olfactory subconscious" and, in anticipation of future research, he stated: "We shortchange ourselves by comparing the olfactory powers of animals with our own conscious sense of smell while ignoring our olfactory subconscious."

An excellent physiologic analogy that he used to explain our sensitivity to odor is modeled on the effect of removing the adrenal cortex that governs our sensitivity to the taste of salt. The adrenal cortex, which is situated above the kidney, produces steroid hormones responsible for the maintenance of our salt balance. Without these salt-retaining steroids, we lose salt and die, unless we can maintain salt intake by intense dietary replacement. In man, the conscious sensitivity to the taste of salt is enhanced by as much as 60,000 times in adrenal insufficiency where those salt-retaining hormones are missing.

Similarly, under the influence of sex hormonal levels, our sensitivity to pheromonal odors may dramatically increase or decrease. Changes in hormonal levels are factors modifying our sensitivity to our environment. In more modern terms, this has been called "state dependency" where the level of one hormone or stimulus determines our sensitivity to another.

Wiener summarized the above as follows: "The idea of chemical messages passing between me and thee, without either of us being aware of them, is a very hard one to swallow – for this reason, it is good to remember that a number of other improbable sounding chemicals of man to man communication have already been discovered or confirmed."

We believe that we humans as representatives of civilized culture, have, in large measure, been intimidated by a societal and religious view which have denied us awareness of our own sexual odors.

When we first began our examination of the role of odor in human sexuality we wondered why human awareness of this appeared to be virtually absent.

This social inability to recognize odor as sexually important developed because it may have been required for the orderly development of civilized conduct between the sexes. We couldn't maintain a functional society if men and women were to compulsively and aggressively chase after one another at the first whiff of a sexually attractive odor. Clearly, as seen in the behavior of cats and dogs, uncontrolled pheromonal responses could disrupt organized social behavior. While to some extent this may be true, we now also see sexual odor repression as having a broad cultural basis that has inhibited frank discussion, to say nothing of investigation, in Western and other societies.

However, not all societies and cultures are so inhibited. Dawn Lamb, in collaboration with June Cleverland, in the late 1930s, explored the jungles between Oaxaca and Chiapas north of the Gulf of Tchuantepec, on the Pacific side of the Mexican jungles. In one village, La Junita, they found the following.

"Dances held during these fiestas are primarily for the choosing of a mate by scent. The Indians believe that since everything in Nature has an odor, human odor is most important: they believe that it reveals sickness, fear, hate, and love, and it indicates sexual affinity. This belief plays an important role in their lives. They say that partners chosen by scent always form lasting unions. Frequently you will hear: "I chose him (or her) because he (she) smelled good.""

They also relay the story that if a woman finds a particular man attractive, she will sometimes ask the medicine man to place some article of her clothing near or in his bed. Wives are said to do this if their husbands show signs of disinterest towards them.

As demonstrated by these customs, these Mexican Indians have largely anticipated the revelations of our text. Why these Indians were so aware of the power of their sexual odors, while we Westerners, with all our knowledge of perfumery denied this aspect of our identity is a puzzle worthy of review.

The human response to pheromones is instinctive. It functions in similar fashion to what we see in newborn babies who mimic the facial expressions of their mothers as an unlearned response. They also smile instinctively in the same manner. This inborn behavior results in mutual exchange of emotional impact and undoubtedly contributes to childhood and adult patterns of social exchange and conditioning.

Increasing your awareness of the role of human pheromones in your life will help you to understand the selection of the one you love, your bonding to family and friends, and sexual behavior such as kissing and other intimate sexual behavior. Having this knowledge will enable you to improve all of your relationships.

Chapter 1

Chapter One

"Our sexual behavior comes dangerously close to that of animals, and it is therefore necessary to make it taboo in order to keep the essential distinction that separates us from them."
— Bernard Acard

"Odors have a power of persuasion stronger than that of words, appearances, emotions, or will. The persuasive power of an odor cannot be fended off, it enters into us like breath into our lungs, it fills us up, imbues us totally."
— Patrick Suskind

"The whole surface of the body is physiologically a sense organ, equipped with billions of receiving stations of peculiar sensitiveness, there is hardly a single part in our periphery from which sexual stimulation could not emanate."
— Magnus Hirschfield

The Nose Knows

Smells are everywhere. They pervade every aspect of our lives. Take, for instance, the irresistible smell of bread baking, the sweet, powdery scent of a baby's head, or the sharp tang of an onion being chopped. Each of these has a distinctive smell. Yet, while we readily accept the role that smell plays in our enjoyment of food, we generally shy away from the notion that smell could play an important role in our sexual choices, behavior, and relationships. We have not fully recognized the importance of olfaction to sexual attraction, patterns of sexual performance, or identity.

Our thesis throughout this book is that although we are aware that the nose is a dominant feature of our face, most of us fail to recognize it as an organ vital to our sexuality, and in terms of evolution, this is important to bonding and social organization. We will explain how the role of olfaction – our sense of smell – is directly linked to why we enjoy kissing and oral sex, and whether we prefer members of the opposite, or same sex. These sexual practices and our sexual identity is heavily influenced by sexual or pheromonal odor communication.

Pheromones are surface related secretions we produce naturally from hormones and they transmit our sexual interest to others in a process that is largely subconscious. These chemical messengers are borne by our body hair and our skin as we shed millions of skin cells daily. In that regard our hair is not only an adornment, but a wick that helps to transmit the odors of our sexual identity and arousal. Pheromones are manufactured when secretions by various glands all over our body and face interacts with the bacteria that live on our skin and body hair. As you walk out into the world – *voila*– you have the capacity to both transmit and detect these chemical messengers. What's amazing about this process is that it is powerful, instinctual and a part of our subconscious that is not entirely understood, so it remains a controversy within the scientific and medical communities. We will examine this scientific debate and provide data to support our belief that despite our pride in being cast in God's image, humans may be more like other animals created by God than previously believed.

One must recognize that "good" smells are chemoattractive: they draw us to its source. "Bad" smells are the opposite, they repel us! A mild smell can be attractive, too strong an odor and we are forced to move away from it. Bacteria and protozoa, one-celled organisms, are no different from us in that chemicals in their environment, attract or repel, depending on concentration and this leads to flight or attraction. Attraction results in feeding or conjugation, which in unicellular organisms is the mechanism of sexual exchange.

Although we consider ourselves to be a "higher organism," distinct from others because of our complex, three-pound brain, we bear evolutionary allegiance to the lowly one-celled ciliated paramecium which with the right chemical concentration in its watery environment, surrenders or is attracted to thrust itself against its neighbor to fuse and exchange micronuclei in sexual conjugation. Are we that different?

Anticipation
Odors provide the environment that frequently, more dramatically than vision and touch, lead us to food, warmth, or to sexual excitation. Alternately, it helps us to face our enemies and for us to seek out a friendly environment. We have been likened to Pavlovian dogs: we salivate to the smell of food with striking anticipation that governs our behavior. This ensures our survival and the quality of our life. Without food we

die; without sex, our species dies. Therefore, it should not surprise us that we may be pre-conditioned by certain odors (such as pheromones) to respond positively to them.

Never having tasted chocolate, its smell produces the desire to taste, and once having tasted, desire and anticipation for tasting more chocolate is enhanced. Life without anticipation is full of dangerous surprises or boredom. Odor provides the pathway for excitement and governs our genetic survival and the bonding to those we love that results in familial structure. It should not surprise us that odor, like vision, voice, and touch, bring us together in sexual contact, where desire, pleasure, and release, like chocolate to our sweet cravings, strengthens our resolve to return to it time and again.

Why we are afraid to smell – or to be smelled

Inasmuch as we often fear the natural smells our bodies are capable of creating – we are also less inclined to admit to noticing and enjoying the smells of ourselves or others. What we will soon discover, however, is that the detection and recognition of these smells also provides us with an instinctual way of literally sensing who might be a suitable lover, business ally, or friend. In many ways, we have been conditioned by social factors including racial and national prejudice that is related to how the other group "smelled."

Culturally, Americans have been known to have a fastidious standard of hygiene that requires we bathe, shower daily, brush our teeth, removing all traces of natural body odors and we wear only clean clothing every day. In other parts of the world, whether in deference to different cultural norms or because of economic or environmental limitations, one's daily toilette is considerably less thorough. A thriving cosmetic and deodorant industry capitalizes on this fear of our natural odors, and we spend up to $1. 4 billion annually to mask these smells using manufactured scents that are deemed more socially acceptable.

Unlike our ability to describe what we see, our vocabulary to describe odors, as contrasted to vision, is much more limited. It was Carolus Linnaeus (1703 – 78) who compiled an exhaustive survey of natural history in *Systema naturae*. He applied the same meticulous detail in identifying and classifying smells in *Odores medicamentorum* (1752).

To his famous descriptive list of animal populations he also provided seven categories for smells, ranging from agreeable to disagreeable. Today, however, we often struggle with our modern English language to describe smells and odors finding it difficult to catalogue the nuance of their meaning.

How and what your nose knows

To better understand how much information we receive from our sense of smell, it will serve us to better understand the mechanics of how the nose functions. The nose comprises two large chambers, separated by the septum. At the top of these chambers are millions of olfactory epithelia where smells are detected. These cells, in turn, send electrical signals to the hypothalamus centered in our brain stem. This area of the brain registers emotions such as anxiety, fear, and aggression as well as bodily functions such as appetite, metabolism, and sex drive. With smell, it is not just the olfactory receptors that are involved as they are bathed in mucous which contain odorant-binding proteins (OBPs) that bring odors to the appropriate receptors that convert them to impulses that impinge on our brain. (*See Diagram 1.*)

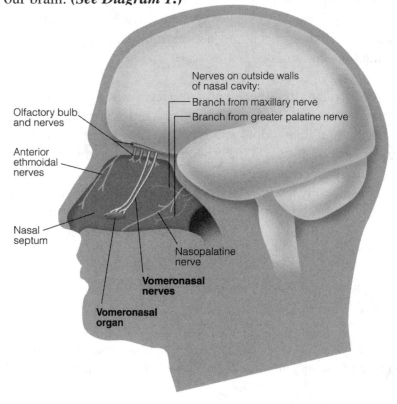

Nerves on outside walls of nasal cavity:
Branch from maxillary nerve
Branch from greater palatine nerve

Olfactory bulb and nerves

Anterior ethmoidal nerves

Nasal septum

Nasopalatine nerve

Vomeronasal nerves

Vomeronasal organ

The nose is comprised of two systems: the main olfactory system (MOS), which is how we identify food odors, and the vomeronasal system (VOS), which detects sexual odors or pheromones, smells that are generated by hormones to influence our sexuality. The main olfactory receptors (MOS) contain an estimated five million cells embedded in nasal mucous. The MOS utilizes cilia in their receptor cells (fine hairs) that distinguish odors such as food.

Independent of the MOS is the vomeronasal organ system (VOS) in which, the vomeronasal organ (VNO) is the center. Also known as Jacobson's Organ, it is located inside the upper pole of our nasal bridge and detects pheromones and ferries this information to the limbic brain (the non-thinking, primitive brain), where sexual attraction and the flight and fight responses are stimulated. The VNO differs from the MOS in that its innervation is distributed via distinct channels on each side of our nasal bridge and have special neural receptors which have microvilli, small projections from their cell surface that are distinct from the hair-like cilia receptors found in the MOS. These microvilli respond to sexually derived odors that interact with our brain stem and frontal cortex.

The exact centers for human sexual response in adults have not been defined except as measured by heightened brain wave patterns that are stimulated beyond conscious awareness as defined by sexual smell (pheromones) as distinct from odors involving food. The VOS in some way must make contact with our limbic, primitive brain that helps us to respond to our social environment. To be "limbic" is to be youthful and the "limbic look" is what you see in the eyes of lovers or two- or three-year-olds, delighted by the discovery of love or their ability to explore their environment.

Jacobson's organ

Jacobson's organ, the key receptor of the vomeronasal system (VOS), contains distinct non-ciliated micro-villous receptors independent of the olfactory nerve. These go to the brain via a separate accessory nerve to a distinct brain nucleus in the amygdala, a part of the limbic center of the brain (Scalia & Winans, 1976) which also involves broader areas in the human brain. Debate continues in the medical and scientific communities as to whether Jacobson's organ, the vomeronasal organ (VNO), is truly functioning or if it's a vestigial organ in human beings that is only active in the human embryo. To further complicate matters, there are experts who say that pheromonal communication, or the awareness of sexual odors, can occur in the absence of a functioning Jacobson's organ. Essentially, the debate centers on how one defines pheromones and pheromonal communication. We will argue that pheromonal communication is made possible by the vomeronasal organ and in humans it still may play a role almost as vital as that seen in the sexual responses of our mammalian friends: cats, dogs, and horses, where the VNO and its VOS connections are more clearly defined, and sexual behavior is outrightly governed by their noses.

First identified by Danish scientist Ludwig Levin Jacobson in 1811, the vomeronasal organ, or Jacobson's organ as it is called, was believed to be a non-functioning organ in humans. However, in the last decade studies have been conducted that strongly suggest that nearly all healthy people have a vomeronasal organ. At the Univ. of Colorado Medical School in Denver in 1991, Bruce Jafek, an ear, nose, throat surgeon and David Moran, a cell biologist and electron microscopist, examined 200 people and discovered that all of them except two had a vomeronasal organ.

In another study at the Univ. of Mexico Medical School, a thousand patients who were seeking plastic surgery were examined, and of that number, in 808, the vomeronasal organ was easily detected. Among the others, 125 patients had deformities of the nasal septum that, once corrected, enabled the doctors to see the vomeronasal organ in all but 23 patients. Jose Garcia-Velasco concluded in this survey, that the vomeronasal organ is "a normal, distinct structure of the human nose, and is present in practically all subjects studied." Again, the vomeronasal organ, although it anatomically shares its place in the nose, is structurally different from our more familiar main olfactory system (MOS) that detects food odors. Both the vomeronasal and main olfactory systems touch related areas of the brain, but their functions are distinctly different. In that regard our sense of smell is engineered by a cluster of cranial nerves, including the vomeronasal (VOS); the main olfactory nerve and its olfactory bulb (MOS); and the trigeminal nerve. (See Diagram 1.)

Anatomically, in addition to the more widely recognized VOS and the MOS, we are now beginning to recognize the importance of a fourth distinct olfactory pathway. This is the "terminal nerve" (*nervus terminalis*) which was first described in sharks. This nerve is responsible for sexual behavior, governed by the release of lutenizing releasing hormone (LHRH) from the brain. LHRH governs ovulation and/or sperm production in humans. Hormones, which interfere with LHRH, are currently being used to stimulate or control fertility and, when blocked, to treat prostate cancer in men and precocious puberty in children. LHRH releases the lutenizing hormone (LH) that governs sperm and egg formation. The developing VNO exports LHRH to the brain hypothalamus from its developing site in the embryo's nose. Responses to these gonadotrophic hormones increase with sexual maturity and with the onset of menopause in aging women and andropause in aging men decrease. In regard to the above, the terminal nerve is also an odor receptor, but its functional presence in mammals is still open to question.

The trigeminal nerve responds to severe olfactory stimuli, such as spirits of ammonia. There are more cranial nerves, central nerves governing the sensory input of our head and brain involved in smell perception than any other communication system. Smell, which influences taste, represents a fundamental survival system going back to the origins of life.

Moran discusses the anatomy and physiology of the VNO and the VOS, and its related controversy, in a paper asking "Are the Surviving Vomeronasal Pits Connected to Responsive Brain Centers in the Adult that Respond to Odor?" There is evidence that there is an electrical brain response to chemically active stimulants called "vomerophorins" in adults. The absence of a well defined brain center, as has been seen in other mammals, these investigators feel reflects on the major evolutionary expansion and adult growth of the human brain where this auxiliary olfactory center, involved in sexual communication, is diffusely hidden, but still functional.

Cranial Nerves

There are twelve cranial nerves that emerge from our upper brain and cord to supply our face and upper body with vital information. Most of us are familiar with the optic nerves, which are necessary for vision. The importance of the sense of smell is apparent in that nature has equipped us with four sets of cranial nerves for odor detection. These are the terminal nerve or "supernumerary cranial nerve" or "zero cranial nerve;" the vomeronasal (VOS) or accessory olfactory system (AOS); the main olfactory nerve and its olfactory bulb (MOS), and the trigeminal nerve. These nerves innervate our noses and have a long evolutionary history.

The trigeminal nerve is thought to be less involved in behavioral responses related to taste or sexual response, but it responds rapidly to dangerous, pungent, or noxious odors, such as ammonia. The trigeminal nerve triggers behavior (withdrawal) distinct from the response mediated by the other three olfactory nerves which communicate with centers of the brain that process odors of food or sex.

Recent clinical research indicates that the human vomeronasal organ responds to pheromonal scent signals without conscious awareness that the odor is being detected. In other words, vomeronasal organ (VOS) sensitivity can bypass the conscious mind and go directly to the subconscious. The VOS provides physiologic expression to the subconscious as it detects the presence of scent and responds reflexively. Like a group of conspirators or gossips, pheromones can work behind our back, profoundly influencing the emotional quality of our lives.

Pheromones

The pheromonal debate centers on three main points: the nature and function of pheromones (how one defines pheromones); the role of Jacobson's Organ and what is required for both the "sender" and the "receiver" for pheromonal communication to occur. Because of the importance of pheromonal communication to our bonding, familial and sexual relationships, it is time to define our terms to make our argument clear.

Pheromones are substances that are secreted by one species that can be detected by another member of the same species and, in the case of sexual attraction, result in physiological changes in the "receiver" that will often result in a reciprocal behavioral response of receiver to sender. This might mean flirting or animated conversation or a desire to draw closer to the "sender" of the pheromone. Jacobson's organ, for our purposes, are represented by twin pits that lead to neural receptors that reside adjacent to the nasal septum and whose function is to detect pheromones – substances derived from our skin or glands that mingle with our sweat, and provide,with the help of bacteria living on our skin, genitalia, and hair provide the odors that are inhaled through our nose.

We believe that the function of Jacobson's Organ is to detect pheromones. Once detected, these odors are translated via our nostrils into chemical transmitting signals that are ferried to our limbic or "reptilian brain." It's here where our emotions including fear and sex drive register and provoke responses that are a key to our survival.

Again, pheromonal communication occurs when a person emits pheromones that are detected and received by another person, who in turn, can respond by drawing near to the sender or rejecting him or her. While responding to pheromones we develop odors of sexual response or attractants governing intimacy, in reciprocal fashion. While this discussion has simplified a number of details, it describes the basic process we believe exists to make human pheromonal communication work. It is a mutual stimulus response system focused on socialization, most frequently evidenced as sexual response, as dramatically demonstrated by sniffing and arousal seen in our pets.

Emotions

Apparently our transmissions of odor may not only involve sexual interaction. Apparently, sweat collected from our axillae may signal how we feel: happy, anxious, or depressed. Jacob and McClintock studied men and women after their viewing standardized films that created moods of happiness or anxiety, these subjects had their axillary sweat then collected and stored in bottles for male and female sniffing. Olfactory observers could ascertain the resultant mood of the subject. If more studies of this type confirm the above, it is obvious that we have to add a new parameter to facial expression, voice, and posture as determining an observer's response to our true romantic or sexual feelings.

When we fall in love many factors come into play: we may be drawn to beauty, strength, intelligence, health, vigor, or the promise of financial security. However, all these factors may be secondary to pheromonal reactions impinging on our subconscious and awaking our limbic brain to sexual desire.

No matter how virtuous the subject of our desire, or our objective evaluation of the one we love, the focus of our love transcends at a given moment our human dignity, based on our rational thinking brain. We must consider, without embarrassment, that, as part of our evolutionary heritage, our lust for the beloved is in many ways similar to the behavior of dogs aroused by a bitch in heat. While extreme, this comparison is a frank assessment and to understand the significance of love and family, we must examine our behavior in response to pheromones in a rational study to understand the influence of the vomeronasal pheromonal system on human bonding and reproduction.

Does our emission of and our response to sexual odors, subconscious or conscious, constitute passion? Does this explain kissing, nuzzling and oral sex? Does this explain the difference between heterosexual and homosexual love? While as humans we have a rational brain, it is our feeling that pheromones not only strongly influence our behavior, but like other primal appetites, such as hunger and thirst, they remind us that sexual attraction is a powerful force that is as complex as it is persuasive and frequently irresistible.

The Pheromonal Subconscious

Pheromone responses reside deep in our primitive auxiliary olfactory lobes. They produce long-term memories separated from our rational perception. Analogously, our disciplined responses to sexually induced odors are similar to speech as an intrinsic element of what makes us human.

Both speech and smell are transmitted through the air. They both develop from preconceived neural circuitry, like the song of the male canary. The canary's warbling and the child's prattle can be influenced by imitation but the child has to be ready to let it out. Similarly, pheromonally-mediated behavior patterns reside within the brain, and like speech, are also difficult to discern until ready to emerge.

What characterizes humans is our speech, and as such, we have the ability to mold its expression. Pheromonal-induced behavior like speech, requires special stimuli to demonstrate it's presence. Pheromones are demonstrable influences only at the chronological point in development that determines gender identity and sexual maturity. It is possible that the hidden expression of pheromonal influences must not be prematurely squandered or expressed until the right stage of sexual maturity if these odor influences are to be successfully utilized in later sexual expression. As it is only now that we can see pheromone influence as a key element in the expression of our subconscious.

Fundamentalists insist that the purpose of humans is to reproduce and populate the world for the glorification of God. What we, as a culture, fail to see is that pheromones provide a strong compulsion to expedite our ability, indeed, our need, to fall in love and form long-lasting emotional bonds that lead to raising a family. Again, as pheromones are stimulating the area of the brain that registers primitive instincts including the sex drive and the flight and fight response, it is not surprising that the sexual pull that draws two people together is at once, irresistible and also, irrational.

The importance of the above in human physiology is the fact that odor response may often be hedonic, a feeling rather than a distinct sensation in that it differs from the familiar instant sensual awareness of touch, sound, or vision. Odor is seen as a Proustian experience, and, unlike visual experience, we cannot as readily bring back odor sensation from memory storage without external aids (Engen, 1982). It is more than coincidence that memory of our sexual experiences suffers from similar limitations that call upon us to repeat the experience resulting in an addictive phenomenon that is only poorly satisfied by memory.

As humans we have developed our civilization over two million years of evolution. Humans, unlike the apes, and other animals, have a hidden estrus (signaling the sexual ovulatory reproductive availability of women). Our women do not signal their readiness for copulation by visible color, as do female baboons. Instead, we feel that odor awareness of fecundity is the attracting but essentially hidden element in our sexual behavior. We act to this stimulus to pleasure and follow with reproduction based on odor clues that govern overt behavior to direct our immediate social actions that sustain our attention to each other? While women have subdued the major visible clues of their reproductive availability, do they sustain remnants of what is so obvious a reproductive odor stimulus to males as seen in dogs or cats?

Is homosexuality an odor preference predetermined by a brain "love map," that signals sexual interaction despite being divorced from anatomic convenience and the genetic necessity for reproduction?

Is oral sex something more than reciprocal pleasure? Does it induce a sensory overload, drawing us together based on an aesthetic subconscious desire for fusion? Do we bathe in a pheromonal olfactory milieu necessary for sexual release. In terms of evolution, was this erotic sensibility directed to reproduction by putting pleasure and pheromonal stimulation as a key principle for species survival? Later, we will examine how odor preferences are central to our sexual identity, sexual preferences, and our passion for certain sexual practices, such kissing, nuzzling, and oral sex.

Limbic System

Under the cerebral cortex—the highly convoluted portion of the brain that gives the human animal its superior intellect and reasoning ability—lies the limbic system. This is our ancient animal brain, which developed far earlier in evolution than did the cortex, the outer layer which governs rational thinking. The limbus is responsible for survival mechanisms associated with social interactions. The limbus translates drives and emotions such as anger, thirst, and pleasure-seeking, into behavior designed to satisfy those urges. We seek food, become aggressive toward our enemies, court a mate. The limbus is the part of the brain that responds to a threat with "fight or flight." It helps us survive by being alert to our environment, mediating social interactions, preparing us for action.

When human beings are turned on, we can see a "limbic look," in the eyes. This is the kind of glow in the eyes which toddlers have when they are curious and interested in everything about them. Teachers can always tell the good students who are interested in learning by the intensity of their gaze. Lovers and religious fanatics have the "limbic look," because they are passionately focused on another person or an idea that substitutes for love. When a house cat stalks a bird or a dog chases a rabbit or a female dog in heat, they have the same limbic look in their eyes.

It is the limbic part of the brain that responds to food and sexual odors. One might call that area of the brain, a bearer of the true subconscious since it acts without conscious awareness to initiate behavior that is critical for individual and/or species survival.

A short history of sexual odors

Historically, Kalegorkis, a psychiatrist, (1963) was among the first to provide a review of olfactory influence on human sexual behavior. He referred to Daly and White, (1930) who first postulated that olfactory stimuli were key elements that prompted changes in our behavior, not unlike the action of a moth being driven to the flame. It is of interest that Daly, a psychoanalyst, worked with White, an entomologist, and their work preceded by many years the extensive explosion in identification of insect and mammalian pheromones.

Daly was among the first to propose the use of odors for psychotherapeutic benefit. He postulated that there is evidence that odors exert a subtle effect that operates directly in the service of reproduction. He also raised the question as to why the conscious recognition of this is so repressed in humans? In this regard, he believed that the recognition of the hypnotic nature of smells in sex attraction were lost to us because of the necessary social inhibition of the sexual impulse as an inevitable result of the strict need to control incest behavior and other behaviors governed by sexual taboos necessary for familial and species survival. Without control of sexual impulses determined by odor, human civilization would be impossible! It is unfortunate that Daly's work was ignored and Kalegorkis failed to get his psychiatric colleagues to focus on the role of odor in human development.

As with Alfred Kinsey, a trained zoologist who was also concerned with insect behavior, it took an individual like White, a biologist operating outside the bounds of psychoanalysis to persuasively posit insect behavior as a model for human sexual patterning as a function of odor. It is of interest that these analogies are still not generally accepted despite the universally accepted validity of pheromonal observations in insects, amphibians, reptiles, and mammals. Ironically, psychiatrists, despite scientific training, have usually preferred to use analogies to explain sexuality based on Grecian mythology rather than using the direct observations readily available to us by using comparative zoological behavioral data.

It has been said that much of the phenomenon of passion in humans would, when stripped of euphemisms, simply represent "a blind response to tropisms" – inborn brain-programmed responses to stimuli that have survival value. In that sense, the human sex drive can be seen as a tropism. If we think that the tropic action of the moth being drawn to the lethal flame is "stupid," think of how many humans have been consumed by sexual passion.

Daly noted that "the study of this subject, i.e. sex, is made difficult in humans by the fact that humans are ever inclined to credit the object which tends to call forth our passion with attributes and powers that emanate from ourselves rather than with those which are inherent in the object." In other words, desire, which we attribute rationally as resulting from our superior intellect, may be no more than an instinctual response to a pheromonal odor emanating from the object that stimulates our craving.

Alex Comfort (1971), the gerontologist, whose sex manual was among the first to openly focus on oral sex, also pioneered in calling our attention to pheromonal influences in human behavior (Comfort, 1975).

Although a pioneer in the study of human sexual behavior, Havelock Ellis (1920) saw odor affinities in relation to fetishism. He felt that the sense of smell was too underdeveloped in humans to be of significance in normal sexual attraction. In contrast, Bieber (1959) said that "the onset of heterosexual reactivity is no more a learned response in humans than it is in dogs." He proposed that between the ages of two and five, the central nervous system developed to the point where it could register arousal in response to sexual odors.

Eroticism in infants involving spontaneous genital stimulation and interest has been described in both sexes. (Bakwin, 1971) Bakwin indicates this in his own case histories and quotes Kinger (1948) where he feels that repeated orgasms are possible at this young age. This is startling and questionable, but in view of this, instead of seeing human behavior developing as outgrowths of oral or anal stages of early childhood development, as popularized by Freud, we feel that sexual preferences in adult life may be better explained by the primacy of body odor which envelops the infant. What Freud describes as a latent fixation on the early oral or anal stages of our development may instead be a normal outgrowth of continuing chemosensory organization based on innate olfactory patterning that develops prenatally or in the early months of our life. In support of this, Ellis thought that genital excitement - i.e., masturbation – could excite the olfactory center. He cited Wilhelm Fliess (1897), a colleague and friend of Freud, who felt that there were areas of nasal tissue with "erectile" properties similar in nature to our genitals. Fliess claimed, while rejected today, that our nasal mucosa behaved similarly to the hormone-sensitive tissue in the vagina or uterus, which responds to the menstrual cycle.

It is of considerable interest that Fliess had a profound influence on Freud and is credited in conveying to Freud his concepts of juvenile sexuality, bisexuality, and repression. How different our understanding of human behavior would be today had Freud, instead of concentrating on the oral, anal, and genital parts of our sexual anatomy (the erogenous zones), focused instead on olfaction (i.e. the odors generated from these parts), as a unifying force governing libido (i.e. sexual desire), in its age-related stages.

It is ironic, that despite Freud's awareness of infantile sexuality and his enthusiastic support of Wilhem Fliess' (1897) concept of the nose as a sexually sensitive (hormone responsive) organ, Freud denigrated the sexual role of odor in human behavior. He classified as "prurient" any sexual interest in odor, which along with masturbation, was considered a "perversion," and such is his influence that these attitudes governing sexuality today, still color much of our thinking.

If Freudian thinking, which has contributed so much to our conceptual ideas regarding human behavior, had given attention to the importance of olfaction, it is likely that we would have long since developed more physiologically grounded concepts of sexual behavior, subject to rational psychiatric therapeutic intervention. The sexual basis of neurosis might then have included a chemosensory focus, (i.e., olfaction), and human behavioral studies would have included major chapters focusing on the role of smell in the practice of psychoanalysis.

Defining terms

There is no doubt that the VNO is present in the developing human embryo where its role might be to transmit luteinizing hormone releasing hormone (LHRH) which is involved in sexual maturity, to the forebrain. However, the existence of a functional VNO in the adult is still questionable to many, although the anatomic crypt-like structures are still present. The question is, are VNO structures in the adult innervated, as they are in other mammals, and sensitive to pheromonal stimulation?

"I don't know why there's a controversy about it," says Avery Gilbert, Ph.D., a sensory psychologist, of the continuing debate around pheromones and pheromonal communication. Dr. Gilbert believes that Jacobson's organ is fully functioning in adults. In the absence of a vomeronasal organ, he says pheromonal communication is still possible. "You don't have to have a VNO. In animal studies it's been shown that blocking the VNO doesn't necessarily disrupt pheromonal communication." We should be aware he says that people who have had nasal plastic surgery (a nose job), may have had it removed unintentionally.

If anything, Dr. Gilbert believes that pheromones are transmitted, somehow, from person to person generated through sexual odors emitted by our skin into the air we breathe. "There are a lot of good examples (of pheromonal communication) we have from studies with rats and other rodents, observations that suggest a priming effect: a scent given off by one rat results in the other rat being physiologically more ready for ovulation." A pregnant female rat responds alternatively to a strange male rat, whose odor can induce a spontaneous abortion leading to a renewed ovulation, resulting in the general advantage to the strange male rat that can now introduce his sperm into a formerly closed gene pool.

In the case of human menstrual synchrony as seen in Martha McClintock's work with women who share a close environment, it implies that there is some kind of cue – something is transported through the air – through breath, skin, sweat, or urine that results in observations that women living or working together have menstrual synchrony, which is a good example of human "pheromonal signaling."

As to whether pheromonal communication occurs if only there is an anatomical functioning VNO, there are those like Dr. Gilbert who, again, are not entirely convinced that this is an absolute physiologic necessity. "Let's say the volatiles (in smell) from one person is reaching another person through (breathing from) an open mouth. By inhaling (a sample of the air that surrounds us), there may be a number of things present including diesel fumes, food, the smell of someone's antiperspirant. Perhaps some pheromones are also present and you're going to get an olfactory experience as well as pheromonal stimulation, but will you be able to tell the two apart?" What's important to note here, however, is that we can be conditioned behaviorally by our response to smells.

How many of us have been conditioned to sexually respond to perfume or even cigarette smoke, which when combined with pheromones, becomes a heady brew. Like Pavlov's dogs, we can also be encouraged to salivate or become sexually aroused through repetitive experiences from exposure to odor or visual cues. For example, how many of us, with a lover that smokes, have been conditioned to the acrid smell or taste of cigarette smoke as one would respond to an aphrodisiac?

In regard to that, Dr. Gilbert suggests that this is how people utilize their ability to emit and receive pheromones , (which) may supercede its original function: signaling sexual interest. "Maybe the deep connection between perfumes, romance, and sexuality is an example we've taken culturally to a different level. We may use our olfactory system further than it was developed for reproduction— we've co-opted the system." What this may mean is that with evolution, pheromones have gone from a primary focus of only stimulating copulation to one of socialization, dispelling aggression and leading to bonding governing family and marriage ties. Does this include the play activity of pre-adolescent boys and girls, where socially, the same sex is preferred until the onset of adolescence?

Dr. Gilbert agrees that the recognition of sexual odors, like any other sensory ability, is highly individual. "You talk to some men who find female body odors incredibly arousing and you realize they may have an incredibly active VNO. There's a lot of variability in odor perception and I think the same is true for pheromonal sensitivity."

Pheromones can regulate, but must be distinguished from copulins. Copulins are the obvious odors of direct genital arousal or copulation. Pheromones represent the function of our true subconscious in that they may not be perceived consciously. It may take repeated experience or the addition of commercial perfumes, or environmental clues to make us consciously aware of odors as a sexual stimulant. Unlike pheromones which can be subconscious and subtle in their action, copulins are self-evident in sexual lubrication and are the least subtle of the pheromones that effect our desire.

Pheromonal communication between people is a controversial subject, so it's not surprising that not everyone agrees with their behavioral importance because it puts us on a level with animals. This is due partly to differing definitions as to what a pheromone is and its role in our behavior, as well as to what anatomic criteria is best suited to "prove" the existence of a functioning Jacobson's Organ. It is a healthy debate that demonstrates both the complexity of human anatomy and physiology, but also our efforts to understand how it affects our social and sexual interactions.

To highlight the differences among scientists in the field, we have spoken to a few who are leaders in olfactory research. "No one has demonstrated that there is a functioning VNO," says Charles Preti, Ph.D., a member of the Monell Chemical Senses Center in Philadelphia and adjunct professor at the School of Medicine at the Univ. of Pennsylvania. Despite the existence of certain studies, such as the one conducted at the Univ. of Mexico Medical School by Jose Garcia-Velasco, Dr. Preti is not convinced that Jacobson's Organ is a fully functioning organ.

"(Nasal) pits don't prove a functioning VNO," he says. While he concedes that menstrual synchrony seen in women's university dormitories, as studied by Martha McClintock in the 1980s and confirmed by others, suggests women may respond to what are called primer pheromones. He says that McClintock's study does not provide solid evidence of VNO-relayed pheromonal communication as a necessary experience. "People argue about menstrual synchrony because there's so much intra-women and inter-women contact. However, I'm looking for a more tangible measure, an endocrinological measure," says Dr. Preti.

In regard to Dr. Preti's skepticism we should be aware that our brain represents the largest "gland" in our bodies. Our brain is chock full of what have been called "neurocrines," hormones produced by the brain. This is represented by pregnenalone and dehydroepiandrosterone (DHEA), which can be purchased in health food stores. We also have their sexually-related metabolites, such as estrogen, testosterone, and androestendiol which are also manufactured by our skin, adrenal glands, ovaries, and testes.

Melatonin, primarily produced by our brain's pineal gland, governs the onset of sexual maturity, as well as influencing sleep patterns. While not a steroid hormone, melatonin is also a neurocrine found in the brain. Is it any wonder, that our behavior may be altered by pheromones that depend on our vomeronasal system that feeds into our brain!

Again, our VNO olfactory sensitivity provides a finger thrust via our nasal passages deep into our brain to modify our behavior and direct us sexually via a more subtle internal touch that compels us to want to respond by literally touching others.

As Dr. Preti points out, and as we discussed this earlier, it was Karlson and Luscher in 1959 who first introduced and defined the term pheromones as "a substance that is secreted or excreted into the environment by one individual, which, on being received by a member of the same species, elicits a definitive behavioral, developmental or endocrine response." Dr. Preti points out that pheromones today are classified generally as *releaser pheromones*, which generate immediate and primarily behavioral responses; *primer pheromones,* which generate physiological (endocrine) responses that result in longer term reactions; *signaler pheromones*, that provide information as to the environment: food, prey, or predator. More recently, a fourth category, *modulator pheromones*, are being studied by people like Martha McClintock, and these chemical signals are believed to change "stimulus sensitivity, salience, and sensorimotor integration" that can penetrate a closed or intimate environment. *Modulator pheromones* affect state dependency, an endocrine response that targets not one special organ but provides for a series of glandular behavioral or developmental responses that result in a cascade of physiologic events. The action of thyroid hormones is an example of state dependency. "State dependency" is not one hormone or one gland, but it involves the totality of our response.

While we believe that most pheromones can be odorless and require a functioning VNO to register the detection of pheromones as a subconscious response, Dr. Preti believes otherwise. To his thinking, pheromones do not need to be odorless, nor do they require the sensitivity of a VNO to be "received." In this regard, we agree that what must first be a subconscious response to a perceived pheromonal stimulus can, with repeated reception cause us to eventually become aware of their presence. Our pheromonal awareness can be conditioned by an early experience.

As an example, later in life one can find oneself exclaiming, in regard to pheromonal awareness: "So that is the significance of what I perceive!"

As an example of the above, as a young child, I used to climb into my parents' bed when they slept in late on a Sunday morning. Suddenly, fifty years later I realized that what I smelled in their bed indicated that they had sex before I intruded on their sleep.

While not convinced of the existence of a functioning vomeronasal organ with neural pathways to the brain, Dr. Preti believes in studies that suggest that Jacobson's organ may be functional during fetal development up to 11 to 16 weeks in the womb, after which, he says the nerves that feed it, atrophy and no longer provide a pathway to the brain. He notes, "One study reports the presence of bipolar cells in the early, but not later, stages of fetal development, suggesting that a vomeronasal epithelium is present only during early embryonic life and regress as the fetus reaches term."

Others voice a similar assessment of the current medical literature regarding Jacobson's organ. "You can find the shell of the VNO in adults," says Charles Wysocki, Ph.D., also of the Monell Chemical Senses Center in Philadelphia, and an adjunct professor of anatomy at the School of Veterinary Medicine at the Univ. of Penn. Dr. Wysocki also argues that the main function of Jacobson's organ may be to carry specific endocrine cells to the brain during early embryonic development, but once this task is completed, he believes the network of (VNO) axons and sensory cells die off. "In early embryonic development, there is an emergence of a VNO whose sensory cells and axons do make a connection to the back of the brain," Dr. Wysocki says. And this pathway allows the establishment of specific cells called GNRH endocrine cells that will later secrete LHRH (lutenizing-releasing hormone) in similar fashion to the shark's "terminal nerve" that affect sperm and ovum production necessary for an individual's reproductive health. Once established, however, these cells and their supporting network degenerate. "At 32 to 36 weeks of gestation, you can't find those cells or nerves," he says.

"Many groups have found (the VNO) but they haven't found the accessory bulb that would be located in the brain." "The original concept of a pheromone was that it is a chemical emitted by one member of the species that resulted in a stereotypical endocrinological response," Dr. Wysocki says of the historical definition of pheromones. Today, however, while we are aware of the complexity of the composition and nature of pheromones. "Pheromones don't have to be single chemicals. They are blends – they are several chemicals. The second thing we've learned about pheromones is that they do not (always) elicit a stereotypical response. Context is very important. For example, if an animal detects a pheromone – and the context isn't appropriate – there is no response." In human behavior this is self-evident. There is a great deal of difference in how men and women interact in socially conservative situations, such as funerals, as compared to how they interact in casual environments, such as parties, where flirting and courtship behavior is more appropriate.

Dr. Wysocki rejects the idea that pheromonal communication between people is triggered by "releaser" pheromones such as those seen in moths. "There are no releaser pheromones for humans," he claims. He believes there is no biomedical literature to support the notion that people could send and receive pheromones that would act as a sexual attractant. We emphatically disagree!

In a survey of the research conducted to determine if adults have a functioning Jacobson's organ, Dr. Preti points to data presented by Trotier where researchers examined 1,842 adults for the presence of a vomeronasal organ. "Their results indicated a VNO opening on both sides of the nose in 13% of people. An additional 26% had an opening on one side only. Repeated observations (at least four times) on different days in 130 subjects revealed a surprising finding: 73% of the group had a VNO pit during at least one observation, but these findings changed from observation to observation. On some days no pit could be found while in others it was readily observed. While these studies suggest the existence of a human VNO, they do not definitively provide evidence of a functional VNO with intact neural connections to the brain. Given the confusion, as to whether a human VNO exists (regardless of the absence of bipolar receptor cells) remains a vexing question. We would like to think future research may shed light on these questions. And this book is an effort to shed light on this controversy based on our own experience and that of a vast but still controversial literature. We feel that "love at first sight" is also supported by "love at first smell!"

In light of his assessment of clinical studies and the few studies that are in progress, Dr. Preti concludes that, "The conservative statement should be that adult humans have two small pits on either side of the nasal septum that fit the description of openings to the VNO. Whether this putative VNO is identical in function to the VNO in other species (such as rodents or New World primates) is not yet known."

After examining the current body of research on the vomeronasal organ, Dr. Preti concludes, "Current evidence suggests the presence, in adults, of bilateral pits on the nasal septum that open into a lumen or sac. Whether these structures are remnants of the VNO remains an open question. As yet, there are not well-defined sensory cells described in adults, nor have there been any convincing descriptions of a connection between a sensory epithelium in the VNO and the central nervous system." Despite his skepticism, we feel that this remains an open question that will continue to be debated as more research is conducted and the awareness of the VNO or a related neural influence increases.

Given the complexity of pheromonal communication, perhaps it should not be a surprise that the debate continues. However, it is our belief that pheromones affect an immediate response (involving what are known as "releaser pheromones") and that this contributes to our social interactions.

Sociobiology

The idea behind sociobiology is that human behavior evolved from that of lower order animals, including insects. One of the best books on this subject is *The Moral Animal* by Robert White, (Pantheon Press, 1994), which uses Darwin's evolutionary theory to explain how we evolved our behavioral and domestic structures.

What Wright and other sociobiologists point out is that our present social condition, both good and bad, is the outgrowth of an evolutionary process that resulted from adaptations to our living together as social animals. These adaptations affected our genetic history and natural selection, making us what we are. This selective process has despite political correctness distinguished women from men, not only physically, but in terms of behaviors that underlie our desire for each other, our fidelity, parenting, and our family structures.

In relation to our own western cross-cultural history, notes Wright, we humans "are oblivious to our deepest motivations" and our religious, largely Christian-based view of ourselves, frequently expresses a "horror of sex." What characterizes religious interpretation of the best in human values is a stress on "self denial, abstinence, taming the beast within." While this is important to our cultural survival, along with "altruism, compassion, empathy, love, conscience, the sense of justice," one has to ask how we developed these values over the two to four million years of human presence on earth.

Differences in sexual behavior between men and women reveals that "Men want as many sex-providing child-making machines as they can comfortably afford, and women want to maximize the resources available to their children." As a socio-biologist, Wright sees this in terms of "mental modules" or as we term them, brain "schemata," inborn behavior where "love of offspring" (the "male parental investment") affects the female choice of mate along with "attraction to muscles" or "status." How this fits in with human pheromonal or odor attraction is speculative, but the evidence we feel supports sexual odor influences as a factor in defining the patterns of male and female behavior.

Pheromones in the insect world

Our knowledge of pheromones in mammals has been based on more than 32 years of research involving our understanding of insect sex attractants. The moth is a prime example of a species studied for the anatomical and biochemical nature of its chemosensory system.

A moth has antennae, which, like our nose, is the primary detecting system designed for recognition of chemical stimuli that governs its behavior. It is of interest that the moth has additional pathways that are found in its mouth. In mammals, there are also several olfactory receptor systems, but they are all located anatomically inside the nose.

The primary sensing organ of the moth's feathery antenna consists of two basal segments involved in movement. However, the key antennal function is in the long segmented flagellum that are the bilateral feathery extensions one sees protruding from the head of the moth. The flagellum has one million separate organelles, the bulk of which are chemosensory and designed to detect odor.

The antenna in the insect is the equivalent of our human nose, and as in mammals, the moth has an antennal nerve that runs to its brain that is the equivalent of our mammalian olfactory nerve. Associated with this nerve in the insect's brain, there are spheroidal nerve clusters (glomeruli) of specialized nerve cells that communicate with the insect's brain centers. As is true in mammals the system for insect olfaction has its distinct functional organization independent of that involved in taste detection. Taste in insects is found in mouth parts, antenna, and feet, depending on the species.

The olfactory sensory receptor organs are called "senilla" and these insect sensors do not differ in their functional role from the organs of Jacobson found in the vomeronasal organ of the nose that is the sexual odor receptor in mammalian species, we feel, including our own.

In moths, pheromone stimulation is processed by large "macroglomerular complexes" which are similar to the nuclei found in mammalian brains. These are the centers in the brain that receive the olfactory stimulation and mediate physiologic responses.

The sensilla receptors respond to specific pheromones of defined chemical structure related to the sex of the insect. However, in moths one can graft embryonic cellular antellal disks of the opposite sex into the developing caterpillar. This can result in an experimentally induced disparity between the antennal sexual olfactory receptors and the brain centers responsible for processing and reacting to pheromones. This insect surgery creates what is called a gyandromorph, an insect whose features bear mixed structural elements of both sexes. In effect, by surgically grafting disparate sex receptors, one creates a "homosexual, or bisexual" insect, although this is never ordinarily seen as a normal consequence of insect development in the wild.

As is true in mammalian vomeronasal stimulation, the insect's excitatory pheromone responses are very specific to the pheromonal odors of the opposite sex. Of interest to mammalian responses to pheromones, receptors can be triggered by particular focused chemical affinities. However, the male insects possess brain nuclei that respond best to the total blend of pheromones produced by the female indicating that there is an integration of responses to odor in the insect brain. The insect's olfactory neurotransmitters are similar to what are found in humans, although the sensitivity of the system to chemical stimuli in insects is thousands of times more active.

For odor to be perceived in the insect, the pheromones are absorbed to hair-like surfaces on the antennae similar to what are found in the sensory receptors of the human vomeronasal system. The odor molecules penetrate the fine cellular hair wall to interact with nerve receptors that trigger the nerve impulses that send the scent signal to the brain.

There are literally almost as many pheromones governing behavior in insects as there are insects. These pheromonal olfactory stimuli are also pertinent to the sexual behavior of spiders, mites, ticks, and crustaceans, such as lobsters and crabs.

Examples of pheromonal attractants governing insect behavior have been described in detail by Jacobson (1972) for a wide range of insect species. A description of how sexual attractants produce their effects is taken from his text, "Male Tergal Glands (situated on the back and exposed by wing raising) in the cockroach serve to maneuver the female into the proper pre-copulatory position which arrests her movement (while she feeds on the tergal gland secretion, or palpates the male's back) long enough for the male to clasp her genitalia." The tergal section not only attracts the female by odor, but she feeds on it as he copulates with her. This is perhaps a parallel evolutionary example of the origins of oral sex.

The male sexual odors of insects are at times strong enough to be perceived by humans. In some cicadae, it has a cinnamon odor; in caddis flies it has a vanilla scent. Attractive substances can be volatile, or adhesive to surfaces, and can consist of scales or waxy secretions.

There are specific anatomic sites, depending on the species, which govern sexual interaction and patterns of behavior, depending on the location of the emitters of these attractive scents. These odors are discharged from sites ranging from the tip of the abdomen to glands on legs, back, or head. As in mammals, odor is not the single stimulus to sexual attraction, as fireflies utilize odor as well as vision to attract each other.

Pheromones as insect signals are not only regulators of sexual attraction, but can stimulate attack and aggressive attitudes, as, for example, in bees. In addition, they provide directional clues to food or dwelling places (i.e., hives or ant hills) or they stimulate nursing behavior in adults to feed pupal embryos or to take care of eggs, as in ants and bees.

The character of the substances that provide sexual stimulation vary greatly. They range chemically from alcohols to aldehhdes and fatty acids, and these substances are not exclusive to insect sex attraction as related chemicals are found to be sex attractants in mammals as well. As an example, butyric acid, which is found in human vaginal secretions is detected by humans at a concentration of 1 x 9 (to the 9th), while honey bees can detect it at 1.1 x 11, representing one molecule diluted in over one billion parts of air or water. A good description of the significance of insect pheromones is seen in the now classic description by Lewis Thomas of female moth attraction, which, with the wind blowing in the right direction, can attract males from miles away.

Insects go through larval and pupal stages of development, the attraction of males to a virgin female can anticipate the pupal insect hatching from its cocoon. This is seen in certain moths and butterflies that anticipate the emergence of their sexual partner. The males gather round to sexually greet the emerging female who has yet to experience the world as an adult.

Pheromones obtained synthetically are now used to entrap moths, cockroaches and other insects as part of pest control. Most recently, the pheromone that attracts the tick responsible for Rocky Mountain spotted fever has been isolated and identified. We will soon have available "tick tricks," or poisonous decoys, that attract the male for a lethal copulation, designed to decrease the tick population in our farms and backyards.

Insect responses to pheromones are obvious in their behavioral effects that are similar to what we see in dogs and cats. For humans, these responses are more subtle, but no less a part of our behavioral sexual relationships.

When we see two people meet and strike up an immediate rapport with one another, we are frequently witnessing the power of pheromonal communication. Sexual attraction involves a number of factors including the exchange of pheromones. One reason why we have learned about pheromones only relatively recently is that much of our initial sexual attraction is based on physical appearance – we like what we see and draw near to the object of our desire. Once we draw near, the subtle but sure exchange of pheromones make it possible for us to become further entranced.

For instance, it is no secret that men, in particular, respond to sexy, physically attractive women. From an evolutionary standpoint, it can be argued that men respond to a woman's prominent hips and breasts in the same manner as baboons or chimps react to the ruddy rump or swollen genitalia of females in heat. In both cases, this was to enable suitable reproductive partners to find one another. What we forget is that this visual sexual signaling is also designed to bring us within closer proximity so that odor can exert its subtle predominance.

The human olfactory system is capable of recognizing hundreds of thousands of smells, a skill that professional perfumers and wine tasters rely on for their livelihood. "Noses," as they are called, can distinguish the ingredients of two to three thousand perfume blends. Stoddard, in the *Scented Ape* (1990) has shown evidence that our sensitivity to volatile odors can be surprisingly more acute than that found in rats. The average person is able to distinguish by odor more than 4,000 chemicals that readily evaporate into the air, including alcohol and acetone. As an example of how our olfactory sensitivity operates at a molecular level, consider how we use hydrogen sulfide, a smelly volatile chemical, to mark cooking gas in order to protect ourselves from asphyxiation or explosion by allowing us to detect the ordinarily odor-free gas emitted by our stoves or furnaces.

Is sexual passion merely pheromones?

In 1930, writing many years before the explosion of knowledge about insect and mammal phermones, as mentioned earlier, Daly, a psychoanalyst, and White, an entomologist, postulated that olfactory tropisms, inborn brain-programmed responses to stimuli that have survival value, can influence human behavior. Daly was also the first to propose the use of odors for psychotherapeutic benefit. He theorized that odors exert a subtle effect which operates directly in the service of the functions of reproduction. These odors are differentiated from coprophilic (fecal) odors. He also raised the question as to why the conscious recognition of sexual odors is so repressed in man? Daly believed that the recognition of the hypnotic nature of smells in sexual attraction were lost to us because the taboos surrounding incest and other sexual behaviors make it necessary to inhibit the sexual impulse.

As mentioned before, in 1963 in one of the first review papers on olfactory influence on human sexual behavior, Kalegorkis, a psychiatrist, used the analogy of "a moth to a flame." Again, it is unfortunate that Daly's work was ignored and Kalegorkis failed to get his psychiatric colleagues to focus on the role of odor in human development.

It took Alfred Kinsey, the chronicler of human sexual behavior operating outside the bounds of psychoanalysis, to make the case for insect behavior as a model for the effect of odor on human sexual patterning. Kinsey was a trained zoologist who was also concerned with insect behavior. Interestingly, these analogies are still not generally accepted despite the universally accepted validity of phermonal observations in insects, amphibians, reptiles, mammals, and even birds. Psychiatrists since Freud, have usually preferred to use analogies to explain sexuality based on Grecian mythology rather than comparative zoological behavioral data.

White summarized the importance of phermones by quoting Howlett on the robotic nature of insect sexual response as analogous to "pouring mint sauce over a pair of boots under the impression that now he was being offered roast lamb."

White felt that "much of the phenomenon of 'passion' in man would, when stripped of euphemisms, simply represent a blind response to tropisms." Daly stated that "man is ever inclined to credit the object which tends to call forth our passion with attributes and powers that emanate from ourselves rather than with those which are inherent in the object." In other words, sexual desire, which we attribute rationally as resulting from our superior intellect, may be no more than an instinctual response to a pheromonal odor emanating from the object that stimulates our craving.

Humans and Dogs

As humans, we believe we occupy an exalted position as compared to dogs, however, we share more than home and hearth. We also share some of the same chemical components found in canine vaginal secretions. We produce valeric acid, as dogs do, a fatty acid that stimulates copulative behavior in male dogs. Human sweat also contains fatty acids that are breakdown products of bacterial action on vaginal or skin secretions or the skin cells that have been shed. (These products are also responsible for the rancidity of spoiled milk or the smell of the uriniferous male goat.)

Marshall et al (1981) showed that dogs have four times the odor sensitivity to valeric acid than people do. Although its concentration is low in human vaginal secretions, the minimum human odor detection threshold for valeric acid makes us capable of being aware of its odor presence at the same level that activates overt sexual behavior in the dog.

Schleidt et al (1981) and Doty (1985) have found that human adults, not unlike the dog, can identify both their own and the odors of the opposite sex. This finding was based on an experiment involving sampling from axillary sweat secretions, which were described by males as "pleasant" when obtained from women and "unpleasant" when obtained from men. What would have been interesting to discover is if the same responses would occur utilizing secretory odors obtained directly from the penis and vagina.

Kloek (1961) showed that a range of steroid hormones, some secreted by our skin, can be quite discernible as odors to humans. Steroid hormones, which include the male hormone, testosterone, and the female hormone, estrogen, as well as dehydroepiandrostrone (DHEA), are derived from cholesterol and are formed in the brain, ovaries, and testes. In addition, many of these steroids are secreted by glands of the skin, especially those of the axilla and genitals.

Chapter 2

"Sometimes I think if there was a third sex, men wouldn't get so much as a glance from me."
— Amanda Vail (1921 – 1966)

"Women from time to time don't have it easy either. But we men have to shave."
— Kurt Tucholsky (1890 – 1935)

My curiosity about and interest in the role of odor in human sexuality began with a number of isolated observations taken from my own life and that of people I knew. All of them are vivid examples of how important smells are to us in creating bonds or severing them. A widow once told me, " I was popular as a young girl and dated many men, but I fell in love with Ed because I liked the way he smelled." Another friend swears to me that he knows when his lover has entered a room before he sees her. Her scent announces her presence. Years after the fact, I can still recall the smell of my seven-year-old girlfriend. The origin of this glorious smell was her sweaty neck, which, in my excitement, I would tickle. This Proustian memory, related to skin and sweat but not genitals suggests that subtle odors can determine early sexual preferences, and in this case reproductive sex was not even in our vocabulary.

While these examples demonstrate how persuasive and tantalizing sexual odors can be, the opposite is also true: exposure to unpleasant sexual/ body odors can be offensive and off-putting. A male friend, who was bisexual, left his wife after three years and resumed his former gay lifestyle. He "lost interest" in her, he said, "because I didn't like the way she smelled." But, he found the odors of his gay friend appealing.

In close quarters, strong sexual odors that are not welcomed become intrusive. A woman physician colleague declares, " If I don't like the smell of a man (and) if he imposes it on me it's an invasion of my privacy, like cigarette smoke in a 'no smoking' zone. Sometimes it is even more intense than that. It is a rape of my boundaries."

Nor is the affinity for sexual odors notable only in adults. Young children are well known for delighting in the smell of their bedclothes and blankets. As the father of six, I was made aware that the smells of a one-year-old's security blanket may be essentially masturbatory. One of my daughters would frequently push her blanket both into her nostrils and genitals and when she awoke, hand it to my wife and I to share as a social gesture. We also noticed how upset our toddlers would become when their blankets or teddy bears were washed and the smell of detergent replaced the smell of their comforting body odors. A woman friend told me that sometimes after she and her husband have sex, her three-year-old daughter will come into their room and rub her face in the pillow and sheets that are saturated with the smells of sex. In this way, even very young children are aware of sexual odors – of their own and others. Sometimes these smells are comforting and reassuring, but again, in other contexts, these odors may be unappealing. As a child, I remember squirming to get free when an overly affectionate aunt or uncle tried to hug me or make close physical contact. Was I trying to escape the odors that their bodies unwittingly gave off?

As we can see from these examples, body odors both draw us in or repel us, depending on the situations in which they arise. Many of us can recall sexual odors from loved ones in our past, and realize now how much these smells played a role in forging emotional bonds with those people who touched our lives.

Again, the importance of the above in human physiology is the fact that odor response may often be hedonic, a feeling state rather than a distinct sensation in that it differs from the familiar instant awareness of touch, sound, or vision. In support of human sensitivity to pheromones and the influence of human sexual odors, although we are not in the same league as dogs, we can detect hydrogen sulfide (rotten egg odor) with a 0.5 ml dispersion in almost a football stadium of air (Engen, 1982).

In this chapter we will discuss why odor preference is central to the formation of our sexual identity and sexual preference. While Freud would have us believe that our sexual identity is a result of the oral, anal stages of development and further, as young children, the need to compete for mother's or father's attention (as seen in the Odiepus and Electra complexes for boys and girls, respectively), we will argue that this may have another basis.

Freud was a man of his times, and not unlike scientists today, formulated his theories of sexual maturation and attraction in a society torn between sexual obsession and repression.

Freud may have disregarded the role of sexual odors in sexual identity and development because to do so would have been to risk being viewed as aberrant and perverse. Placing human behavior as related to sexual desire (libido) was revolutionary enough; to extend his thoughts in regard to libido to human sexual behavior as similar to that of cats and dogs would have closed all avenues of debate at that time.

Sexual identity

Freud believed that human sexuality developed in stages from oral to anal, which began with bonding and closeness with one's mother, which later resulted in competing for her undivided attention. While it may be difficult to accept all his theories in a postmodern world, it is important to examine them again, as they still serve, in many ways, as the foundation for many of our persistent beliefs about human sexuality.

To his credit, unlike many of his early contemporaries at the turn of the century, Freud understood that children are sexual creatures, even calling them "polymorphously perverse." Freud believed "infantile sexuality" was autoerotic as it did not have a "sexual aim" or a "sexual object." "Above all, gratifications originate through the adapted excitation of the so-called erogenous zones. . . The sexual instinct of childhood is therefore objectless or autoerotic."

As a result of his observations, he believed sexual maturation resulted from passing through a range of sexual phases: oral, anal, and phallic. Childhood sexuality was divided into two periods, the first between the ages of three to five years was followed by a period of "latency," and the second that was marked by the onset of puberty. According to Freud, the hallmark of puberty was an increase in libido for boys and its repression in girls, but more importantly, the passionate desire developed, with adolescence, for a "sexual object." Unlike infantile sexuality that was often masturbatory in nature and autoerotic, he believed that puberty signaled the arrival of forbidden fantasies, often based on parental figures. In contrast to Jungian psychiatry with its inherited archetypes, he believed that early experience governed later behavior. As Freud put it, "Object selection is first accomplished in the imagination, for the sexual life of the maturing youth hardly finds any escape except through an indulgence in phantasies {sic}; that is, in ideas which are not destined to be brought to execution. In the phantasies {sic} of all persons, the infantile tendencies, now re-enforced by somatic emphasis, reappear, and among them one finds . . . the sexual feeling of the child for the parents. Usually this has already been differentiated by sexual attraction, namely the attraction of the son for the mother, and of the daughter for the father." Resolution of these "infatuations" occurs only through a painful tearing away from the obsessions of youth. Nowhere does Freud see sexual attraction or fantasy as mediated by odor.

Fantasy

During the roller coaster of adolescence, a burgeoning sex drive often leads to erotic fantasies and masturbation, both "safe" expressions of a budding sexuality. What helps to create an erotic fantasy? What leads teen-agers to make heroes of Hollywood stars or rock or sports figures? Culturally, boys find it easier to fixate on the bare flesh exposed in men's magazines, while girls may be influenced by the timbre of voice, athletic prowess and other signs that they associate with masculinity. During my puritanical formative years, magazines such as National Geographic offered the exposure of bare breasts in place of Playboy magazine. One must ask, do pheromones play a role in these fantasies? Do our own or related pheromones in the environment help subtly to give rise to aspects of our erotic fantasies?

In our teens, a normal sex drive is present beginning at the age of 13 for girls and age 15 for boys, give or take three years. Today, however, influences including nutrition and cultural changes are clearly accelerating this maturation process and it is not unusual for younger children even before evident adolescence to show a marked interest in sex or to have fantasies such as crushes on classmates of the opposite sex.

The exception to this is precocious puberty, that, with the production of androgenic (male) hormones, there is an acceleration of erotic fantasies that can occur in children of both sexes before the age of six years. Again, what triggers these fantasies? It is worth noting that for boys, it is during pre-adolescence that there is the most male-to-male contact. One can wonder if this male influence on a young boy may influence later sexual orientation, such as a predisposition to homosexuality. To date, there does not seem to be any evidence to show that this is so. Likewise, there are no studies that examine the influence of pheromones and the role they play in our erotic sexual fantasies governing our developing sexuality during adolescence, and our sexual preferences later in adulthood. In the future, it would be interesting to explore the role that pheromones may play in fantasy and if this does influence the choices regarding sexual orientation in adulthood.

Even in close relationships between children and their parents, during this stage of budding sexuality with the tsunami explosion of sexual hormones, teens entering adulthood will often shun the company of their parents, now newly distasteful to their central place in the life of their maturing children. Freud did not see the notion of sexually-related hormones influencing the inborn sexual behavior of children as seen in the "love maps" described by Money wherein sexual preference and patterns of behavior are inborn although environmentally mutable. Our position, however, is Jungian in its concept in that we believe that our sexual preferences represent innate patterns of behavior that mature under sex hormonal influences but are genetically predetermined to be released by the appropriate visual stimulus or pheromonal influences.

We must ask, at what age do these patterns of behavior begin? Like Freud, we believe they begin in early childhood, which means that although we do not accept Freud's concept of oral or anal fixation, we see sexual identity as formed in utereo and which finds its later expression in pheromonal and visual appeal.

Although Freud grasped the concept of hormonal modulation that affected sexual maturity, he didn't see this as an essential factor in sexual preference. Unfortunately, he believed that preoccupation with sexual odors was "sick," on par with leather and foot fetishes. Of course, now we see that the preoccupation with leather or feet can be governed by their smell that acts as a sexual releaser. What we are saying is that we are no different from pea hens aroused by the peacocks brilliant display of tail feathers: while physical appearance is important and we are "turned on" by sexy flashing eyes, or the alluring appearance of beautiful hair, firm muscles, genitals, and shapely breasts and hips, we feel that sexual attraction also requires the presence of sexual odors to bring about the arousal and passion that draws us together.

When does sexually-stimulating behavior cease to be "perverse?" It is well to remember that in China there was an obsessive erotic preoccupation with feet, as was seen in the mutilating, painful foot-binding that altered the lives of generations of Chinese women from the 12th century to the early decades of the 20th century. While the impact of abnormally small feet in women was seen to possess visual appeal similar to the high heels worn by modern Western women, or the pointed toes of the ballet dancer, foot binding, in addition, provided an olfactory stimulus of distinct appeal to the men that encouraged this almost 1,000-year-old Chinese indulgence until 80 or 90 years ago. Men fondled, kissed, and doted on these miniature feet. Those who objected to this sadistic practice were undoubtedly called "perverse" troublemakers.

We believe that Chinese foot binding is a dramatic example of how fashion can be governed by an odor fixation in those that set the fashion. It would be of interest to determine if there was a relationship between sexual fixation on a miniaturized female foot and oral sex. Did Chinese men enjoy both or one at the expense of the other?

Smells that are offensive to most people may be appealing and even sexually arousing to a few others on the same physiologic basis, as seen in the example of pheromones. For example, androstenol, "boar scent," a male pig hormone found in a boar's saliva that sexually excites the female pig, is also found in human sweat. Androstenol is clinically perceived as unpleasant by most men but can be an acceptable odor likened to perfume by many women. An obvious question relates to how androsterol impacts on homosexual odor preference.

The Renifleur
Despite Freud's prudery, he was astonishingly close to understanding the olfactory modulating concept of sexual behavior. In a letter to his colleague, Fleiss, a nose and throat specialist, he wrote: "Olfactory substances, as indeed you yourself believe, and as we know from flowers, are breakdown products of sexual metabolism and would act as stimuli to both these organs (nose and genitals). It would have to be decided whether these act on the nasal organs through the expiratory air or through the blood vessels; probably the latter." Fleiss was convinced that the nose behaved under hormonal stimulation, much like a sex organ, and that nasal mucus was cyclically under hormonal control (as seen in menstruation). Although Fleiss influenced Freud's concepts of juvenile sexuality, neither of them saw sexual preference or oral sex as governed by the response of nasal receptors that are essential to sexual performance and identity. While on the verge of realization, neither Freud, nor Fleiss

saw pheromone odor as a sexually determined factor in sexual identity or sexual preference.

At another point, Freud went so far as to use the term, *renifleur*, to describe "one who is sexually aroused or gratified by odors." Now, no longer seen as a perversion, this revolution in odor awareness has shown us that this aspect of human behavior, far from residing in a perverse few, may be in large measure what much of human sexuality is all about. Indeed, it is unfortunate that Freud missed the significance of his own observations. In view of the common practice of oral sex among half of our American teen-agers, are we to consider them or their behavior "perverse?"

Freud apparently also recognized that bacterial action played a role in providing the scents necessary for olfactory stimulation derived from sexual secretions. Again, it is the bacterial action on the products of skin and the breakdown of sexually-produced lubricants that are responsible in large measure for our sexually-defined odors. Pheromones in mammals resemble the perfumes of flowers, although, unlike flowers, instead of attracting insects to aid in providing pollen, mammals seek to attract a member of the opposite sex of their species for direct action.

The relationship between the scent of flowers and their place in human sexual attraction has been for centuries seen as part of our romantic literature. In *The Marriage of Cadmus and Harmony* (Vintage International, 1993), Robert Calasso gives us a window into the relevance of Greek mythology as it focuses on the central place that odor has in sexual life:

"But how did it all begin? A group of girls were playing by the river, picking flowers. Again and again such scenes were to prove irresistible to the gods. Persephone was carried off 'while playing with the girls with the deep cleavages.' She too had been gathering flowers: roses, crocuses, violets, irises, hyacinths, narcissi. But mainly narcissi, that wondrous radiant flower, awesome to the sight of gods and mortals alike."

"Thalia was playing ball in a field of flowers on the mountainside when she was clutched by an eagle's claws: Zeus again. Creusa felt Apollo's hand lock around her wrists as she bent to pick saffron on the slopes of the Athens, Acropolis. Europa and her friends were likewise gathering narcissi, hyacinths, violets, roses, and thyme. All of a sudden they find themselves surrounded by a herd of bulls. And of those bulls, one is dazzling white, his small horns flashing like jewels. The princess makes so bold as to climb, like an Amazon, on his back. With a show of nervousness, the bull approaches the water. And then it's too late: the white beast is already breasting the waves with Europa up on top."

How does one interpret this? Calasso says "there is no such thing as the isolated mythical event, just as there is no such thing as the isolated word. Myth, like language, gives all of itself in each of its fragments." What is there about the virgin that tames the wild unicorn? Why do the gods associate flowers with their desire to abduct maidens, and what holds Europa to her priapic bull?

Greek mythology perhaps explains itself in Calasso's description of love: "encouraged by his lover's alluring words, could lead to the desired exchange of graces, to the moment when the lover will breathe 'intelligence and every other virtue' into the mouth and body of his beloved. Remember, *eispnein*, or to 'breathe into,' is first and foremost the lover's prerogative." *Eispnelos*, "he who breathes into another," was another word for "lover." This description of one who "breathes into another" is perhaps among the best recorded expressions of the influence of pheromones on the expression of human love.

The influence of floral odors that accompanies the passion of those supernatural lovers who abduct maidens is perhaps a metaphor for the natural body odors, pheromones and copulins that promote desire. In support of this, there is evidence that floral odors are chemically homologous structures that resemble our own pheromones and are capable of stimulating our vomeronasal sexually responding olfactory system. The perfume industry has been largely built on this belief.

Were the actions of the Greek gods any different from the actions of men today? Let's look at an example of male sexual enjoyment when saturated by the smell of women as expressed crudely but effectively in this example of contemporary pornography:

"The thought of not being able to smell one another, to handle each other' sex parts, to lick and tongue into the satiation they had both known would be unendurable.

There was a smell all over the room, it was a womanish smell. All hot cunt, and then he saw Jill's hairs were beaded with her love juice . . .

"Was that what it smelt like when two human beings fucked together? . . . what happened? What did they do to each other?"

This excerpt is taken from *Piece of Tail*, by Sondu Greco, (Continental Classics, 1969). The references to odor are all male-focused. A typical example of male- focused heterosexual pheromonal enthusiasm is also seen in Del Marks' *Deep Thrust*, (Midwood Press, 1977) below.

"So fragrant. My mouth filled with hot slobber as I drank in the fine, foxy, female scent," reads one passage. Pheromones are in the air and everywhere in this explicit depiction of sexual foreplay and intercourse. " The smell of her aroused sex, so fine and musky sweet—yet tinged with a raw, ball wrenching funkiness ransacked my sinuses."

The "Primitive Brain"
When we are highly aroused by sexual smells, these odors are traveling directly to our limbic or "primitive brain." It is here that instinctual drives such as hunger, thirst, and the sex drive are stimulated.

As humans, we respond to, embrace, or reject the odors that stimulate the chemosensory olfactory pattern that has been genetically preprogrammed and mapped within our brain. The olfactory center of our brain is a primitive evolutionary survivor of what is the dominant hemisphere (by size) in lower animals, like lampreys and fishes. Those whom Freud called "renifleur" passionately respond to trophic stimuli providing that primitive input provided by odor, that may be beyond cortical control of the rational brain. In that regard, perhaps we are all like Greek gods, responding definitively if only momentarily to smell.

If we look at animal behavior, a dog in response to a female (bitch) in heat, does not rationally focus his interest looking for a more opportune time to exercise his sexual desire – it is *now*! *Odor*, warms his brain, and directs his attention to copulation. While we have rational and cortical control of the above instincts, we basically are subject to the same pathways.

In regard to the above, involving skin, beyond our cognitive brain, but recognizing its hormonal influence, acne is a complication of the sebaceous oil glands getting plugged and/or infected. These glands are under hormonal control and are found on eyelid, face, armpits, chest and pubic regions involving sexual organs or contiguous with them (Mykytowycz, 1985; Doty, 1985). Boosting a multimillion industry that rivals that for the perfume industry, the furious purchase of products designed to clear teen-aged skin is surely a harbinger of their blooming sexuality and the influence of pheromones on their interactions with each other. And, as the production of sexual hormones roller coasters, so too does the emotions of first loves and broken hearts. As any parent can attest, the dramas behind their sons' and daughters' early relationships are no less real than that what occurs in adults.

While at a younger age, boys and girls may have avoided the other sex because of group identity: For a critical time period, the other sex has "cooties," once they reach puberty, a new interest in the other sex blossoms. "Until girls and boys are three or four, a structure in the hypothalamus called the gonadotropin-releasing hormone pulse generator ticks and tocks and secretes tiny bursts of reproductive hormones," says Natalie Angier in her brilliant work, *Woman*. As Angier points out and as many parents can tell you, toddlers have an insatiable curiosity about their own and others' bodies. But during primary school years as sexual hormones are less prominent, this interest is less so. By the age of 10, Angier notes, the adrenaline and the small amount of sex hormones secreted by the adrenals and gonads in both sexes help to spur our curiosity in the opposite sex. In another few years, the hypothalamus, or key limbic brain center, is "reactivated," once again cyclically firing off more hormones. She notes that in the case of girls, it seems that once a girl attains adequate body fat, she is likely to begin menarche and her ovaries will begin producing healthy levels of estrogen and progesterone. For both sexes, it will be a few more years before the production of sex hormones increases in direct relationship to the number of hours spent talking on the telephone or time spent preening in front of the mirror daily. What teen-agers are experiencing is the heady discovery of each other as potential (whether fantasy or not) boy and girl friends.

Sensitivity to sexual odors

In addition, with adolescence to these obvious signs of sexual maturation, it is our contention that sensitivity to sexual odors is also at work in all of these dating rituals that our maturing sons and daughters are experiencing. In concert with the river of sex hormones that are coursing through our teen-agers' bodies, is their already established ability to detect odors – including sexual odors. While as older adults we may lose our awareness of this as a factor in human sexual contact, it is blossoming in our children as they achieve sexual maturity.

Sweating

Again, the nature of sexual odors is such that there are a number of ways of detecting them. Sweating is clearly part of sexual intercourse, but we do not know if it affects pheromonal dissemination. Perspiration during sex can be both the result of an emotionally stimulating event and/or the result of the weather (heat) or basic physical activity. As we rub body against body, are we sharing our odors in a mixture of combined sexual secretion in which odor stimulation plays a major role?

In addition to sweat, and cutaneous oil secretion, mucous is another factor in pheromonal secretions. Mucous coats the cutaneous smell receptors in our nose. Mucous is chemically similar no matter where it is produced, and we can reasonably assume that if it absorbs the odors necessary for olfaction in our nose as it may also do at other sites. It is logical to assume that sexually produced mucous, and pre-ejaculate — i.e., the genital secretions produced by sexual activity – serve, not only as a lubricant to decrease penile friction, but may also be an odor fixative, holding sexual odors to our body surfaces and thus enabling less volatile odors to get to our nose via touch or taste through dissemination via adherence to our skin.

The mucous sheet that covers the main olfactory epithelium which is 4-5 cm square in size, in our nasal area, may be a significant factor in dissolving odorants to make them more readily available to the olfactory receptors. Vaginal secretions and male pre-ejaculate and semen contain mucous secretions the same or similar to that found in the nose.

There is a cycle that affects our olfactory receptors. Mammals regenerate nasal olfactory receptors; in mice this occurs at six week intervals. Hormonal effects on nasal mucous could possibly act to dissolve or transport odors as well as through a direct effect on the olfactory receptors themselves. (Turn of the century, Fleiss was on to something!)

Sexual preferences

Again, despite good evidence to the contrary, up until recently, anatomists and most physiologists supported the notion that odor was not important in human sexuality because they thought that we lacked, except in vestigial form, the scent sensitive vomeronasal anatomy critical to mammalian sexual behavior. It is our feeling that now that we know that we are very similar to our mammalian cousins and that we are subconsciously aware of these scents, we must re-evaluate our sexual behavior as odor mediated. What we share with our mammalian relatives is a hormonal mediated pheromonal sensitivity that governs our sexual choice and identity.

Homosexuality

How does one explain the presence of homosexuality that appears to occupy six to seven percent of Western society where under the banner of freedom of expression, gay people are continuing to feel more comfortable expressing their true sexual orientation. Lesbian or male homosexuality, or bisexuality, can be explained best by odor preference: in the case of homosexuality, it may be a matter of a shift to the left or to the right of an odor-conditioned love map directed to the propagation of our gene pool. Homosexuality can be seen as a dysphoria where our anatomy is disparate from the archetypical "odor maps" governing sexual performance that directs our attention to reproductive sex. Oral sex is not just motivated by mutual pleasure but by an odor, aesthetic that draws us together!

No studies as to odor preferences of homosexuals as compared to heterosexuals have been reported and it is important to our understanding of sexual preference that these studies be made! Do gay people respond only to the pheromones of members of their own sex?

Because of the absence of any systematic study of homosexual odor preference, a great deal of further work is necessary. Is it possible that homosexuality could be the odor equivalent of what Freud characterized as "juvenile polymorphous sexuality": is it possible that maturity of pheromonal attraction has been denied in homosexuality and pheromones thus may affect male or female gay people without regard to firm sexual identity or conditioning? In this regard, male or female sexual smells could be equally stimulating or directive regardless of sexual identity. Or is homosexuality a definitive choice based on an odor pheromonal love map that is anatomically separate from reproductive reality? In this regard, heterosexual preference for oral sex is motivated by the same sex passion governed by odor preference we see in the homosexual and the same can be said for anal interest as well. Pheromones govern the same genital or anal fixation.

Odor

Humans are generally able to distinguish between the sexes by smell alone and to identify their own odor and that of their mate. These odor distinctions can be extinguished by hygienic measures to reduce apocrine (sweat) odor (Schleidt, 1980). According to Schleidt, personal odor distinguishes between "I am a man" or "I am a woman." While personal identity is important, in the crowded conditions of our society, it is best that odor overload be kept to a minimum. In contrast, in the setting of the dining room, dance floor, bedroom, or its equivalent, our odor identity, perhaps abetted by appropriate perfumes, be given free reign for pheromonal expression to bond us both sexually and in friendship with our loved ones.

Obviously sexual arousal alters our perception and interpretation of what we smell. According to Doty (1985) women surpass men in their odor sensitivity by a factor of 35% when identifying odors in both forced choice and free recall test situations. This discrimination is seen in both pre- and post-pubertal ages (Doty, 1985). Doty anticipated the rediscovery of the physiologic importance of the human VOS, as he felt that this sex difference in olfactory identification suggested that humans may have the potential to communicate sexually via smell.

Consider, for example, dancing, as a way that demonstrates how pheromones allow us to communicate with each other through sexual odors in a socially benign way. While dancing, you respond visually to your partner. However, literally within arm's reach, you are close to one another and you are able to explore the other person by touch and by smell. Holding your partner in your arms, you are close enough to detect and send pheromones! Also, dancing is a physical expression of athletic prowess as well as grace and skill, but what's most important is that, regardless of dance styles, face to face, you have the opportunity to draw the other close, and it is within this intimate exchange that you are able to let the VOS do its work.

Touch me, thrill me

Another way to affect sensory receptors is by erotic stimulation. For example, studies have shown that vaginal stimulation of rodents results in activation of limbic brain centers that impinge on that portion of the brain responsible for odor awareness; this can be measured. In extrapolating this type of response in humans, we know that touching one's own genitals is distinctly less enjoyable than having someone you love touch them. Similarly, because the odor of the one you are attracted to is erotically pleasant, it accentuates the sexual quality of the relationship. Homosexuality in mammals can be seen as a loss of pheromonal specificity when sexual drive and tactile pleasure overwhelms pheromonal reproductive preference.

In a further example, regarding the reception of touch, scratching the afflicted area thereby producing a combination of pain and pleasure, affords some relief by alleviating itching. However, areas of itching induced by allergy can be made to feel pleasurable by applying almost scalding heat, which is most uncomfortable to normal skin. Similarly, in the throes of sexual passion, sensations that to the individual are normally unpleasant, frequently become acceptable or even pleasant. In passion, as in the dark, our sexual preferences can develop because pleasure synchronizes with, or overwhelms odor preference.

Smelling like a rose
In love, with kissing and sexual arousal, men get hard and women become moist. How difficult is it to withdraw and postpone what is so persistent and so important to the maintenance of our species? What is there about kissing that can create this overwhelming desire?

We kiss our close relatives only with ceremonial effect. As children, kissing is viewed as being "gross." The answer has to be vomeronasal: odor, pheromonal attraction demonstrates our affinity to our domestic pets. Our evolutionary allegiance to our primate relatives exists. Apes express our behavior clinically but with the additional urgency for their immediate need for reproductive timing. In apes ovulation is a necessary physiological adjunct to sex, for humans, ovulation is not necessary.

How sweet of God to have given us this universal sexual pleasure unrestricted to season or time of the month. The hidden estrus, the ready availability of female sexual interest provides us with bonding that creates the family. Women do not ordinarily flaunt their sexual availability as seen in apes or monkeys. This allows civilization to flourish without chronic male rivalry or gross competition for females. By turns alluring, comforting, and compelling, the familiar smells of the ones we love help bond us to them. Our family structure is based on our ability to channel our sensitivity and attraction to sexual odors and the demands of society to control our sexual impulses.

Our scientific neglect of odor as a factor influencing our efforts to define gender identity and behavior relate to our lack of awareness of the degree of human sensitivity to odors. As discussed earlier, recent work indicates that the human VOS distinguishes sexual odors dependent on its origin governed by gender. Our sensitivity to these pheromones depends on both its sexual origin and on the sexual identity of the subject smelling it. Regardless of age, our nose contains pheromonal receptors which stimulate brain centers responsible for sexual awareness and sexual identity which mature largely with adolescence. In this we are no different physiologically from animals such as cats and dogs.

If we see our sexual behavior as related to odor we can understand the preferences of homosexuals, transvestites, transsexuals, and perhaps, even fetishists. More importantly, it explains sexual passion. How do we explain the interest in anal sex or our growing national enthusiasm for oral sex? Both of these interests can be divorced from fecal or urinary odors and related to the sexually active glands in the vicinity of the rectum or genitals. It is our feeling that although our changing patterns of sexual behavior may be influenced by pornography, our behavioral responses are instinctive. In order for popular culture to accept non-reproductive sex, there has to be an underlying physiologic basis where pleasure or aesthetics predominate. We believe odor preference is the centerpiece of sexual identity defining sexual preferences and performance.

Odor preferences: The Nose

Again, while we agree that children are sexual beings, as Freud noted, we believe that sexual identity is strongly influenced by odor preference. Again, simply put, we select partners that "smell good" to us. As Freud correctly points out, as children we are not seeking an erotic partner, and while much of childhood sexuality is self-centered: children seek out those that make them feel comfortable or feel good.

In regard to the development of the human nose, Short, in his discussion of "sexual selection and the descent of man," quotes Julian Huxley who called the nose "the physiological penis" as it results in "facilitating the discovery or recognition of one sex by the other."

Apart from anatomy, one has to study our subjective responses to odor. Myktowycz (1985) comments that socially we may be rationally unaware of the odors that characterizes the environment in which we grew up, and to whose odors we contribute.

Pheromonal evaluation is not subjectively reported, but its response can be measured by blood pressure and electroencephalographic changes, with no overt odor awareness demonstrated in the subject. The stimulated subject responds physiologically but has no cognitive awareness of odor.

These subconscious responses are based on vomeronasal stimulation exclusively, as those compounds of pheromonal origin do not stimulate the main olfactory system. Of particular interest to the sexual role of pheromones in humans is the specificity of the response. You need human derived or closely related compounds to get a response. There is also a sexually differentiated sensitivity, depending on the pheromone administered. Only human derived odors, as compared to animal-based pheromones, produce the best response.

As discussed in our previous chapter, people are equipped with odor-producing glands in similar fashion to other mammals (Doty, 1981 & 1985). Again, apocrine, sebaceous, or moisture-producing eccrine glands are present under the arm, in the groin, and on the eyelids, face, and breasts, especially the nipples (Doty, 1981; Labows & Kligman, 1982). Apocrine glands are distinguished from eccrine glands in that they secrete protein or mucous cellular breakdown or secretory products while eccrine secretion (sweat) is essentially of water and salt composition. The eccrine glands, like the kidneys, control water and salt balance. Sebaceous (oil) glands are present on forehead, face, scalp and hair roots. All points of exit from the body, as well as the nipple, prepuce, and anogenital areas (Doty, 1981). There are ethnic, sexual, and age-related differences in odor-producing body areas, governed by the number of glands distributed in the skin. For example, the Japanese have fewer apocrine as well as eccrine glands then do Caucasians.

Sexual maturation

Adolescence is the key time for odor development, as apocrine or sebaceous glands, in large measure, do not fully develop functionally until that age. With the onset of puberty, teenagers typically suffer acne and require anti-perspirants, deodorants, and cleansing creams. During adolescence the production of sex hormones takes off, and in girls, menarche occurs between the ages of 10 to 15 with an even earlier onset in some, perhaps influenced by phytoestrogens (plant estrogens or via hormones that are given to farm animals and end up in our food supply and environment).

With adolescence, estrogen and progesterone female sex hormones are flooding a girl's body, her uterus swells to accommodate an egg and then sheds its rich lining each month if it does not receive one. Her breasts fill out, while her hips widen and preoccupation with appearance and boys may predominate. Similarly, boys will probably experience a sudden overwhelming preoccupation with all things related to sex, shaving, masturbation, and physical prowess. And, as testosterone production surges in boys aged 13 to 18 so, too, alas, does the production of sebaceous oil secretions that often result in the bane of teens everywhere: blemishes and pimples. Although disfiguring for some, this "juiciness" is the hormonally-related moisture that is the trigger to pheromonal production. In regards to the above, acne is a complication of the sebaceous glands getting plugged and/or infected. These glands are under hormonal control and are found on the eyelids, face, armpits, chest, and pubic regions involving sexual organs or contiguous with them (Mykytowycz, 1985; Doty, 1985).

Boosting a multimillion-dollar industry that rivals that of the perfume industry: We have the furious purchase of products designed to clear teen-aged skin that is surely a harbinger of their blooming sexuality. And, as the production of sexual hormones roller coasters, so, too, does the emotions of first loves and broken hearts. Again, as any parent will attest, the dramas behind their sons' and daughters' early relationships are no less real than what occurs in adults. It is our contention that sensitivity to sexual odors is at work in all of these dating rituals that our maturing children are experiencing. While as adults we may lose our awareness of this as a factor in human sexual contact, it is blossoming in our children as they achieve sexual maturity.

In concert with the river of sex hormones that are coursing through our teen-agers' bodies, is the already established ability to detect odors – including sexual odors. While at a younger age, boys and girls may have avoided the other sex because of social pressure and disinterest ("cooties"), once puberty sets in, a new interest in the other sex blossoms. Why?

Sensitivity to sexual odors
Schleidt (1981) and Doty (1985) have found that people, not unlike their dogs, can identify both their own and the odors of the opposite sex. This finding was based on an experiment involving sampling from underarm sweat secretions, which were described by men as "pleasant" when obtained from women and "unpleasant" when obtained from other men. What would the responses have been if the odors had been obtained from our genital areas, such as from the penis, the vagina, or groin of the opposite or same sex? Would these findings hold true qualitatively as a factor determining the male or female choice of homosexuals? Or perhaps, contribute to our desire for oral and anal sex?

Again, Kloek (1961) showed that a range of steroid hormones are discernible as odors to humans. Steroid hormones, which include the male hormone, testosterone, and the female hormone, estrogen, are derived from cholesterol and formed in the brain, ovaries, and testes via pregnenalone and DHEA. In addition, many of these related glands of the skin secrete steroids, especially those found under the arm and on the genitals. Studies should be done to ascertain whether people, like pigs, can be sexually influenced by steroids (sex hormones) found in saliva or skin secretions. "Boar scent" is a hormone secreted in the male pig's saliva that sexually motivates the female.

While Freud has written that the pressure to sublimate or repress our sexual instincts prompts the period of juvenile latency, where sexual activity is minimal, it is only with the onset of puberty that the child actively progresses in sexual development. We believe that it can be argued that the crystallization of sexual identity and sexual preferences is a continuum influenced by the input of pheromonal output and with childhood we are aware of these odors which have not been given credit for juvenile interaction that include periods where girls and boys go their separate ways.

In support of this, new research has shown that there is gender distinction to odor sensitivity that may begin at an early age: girl babies in contrast to boys, respond to odors placed on their rattles at ages as early as three to five months. As humans, we have always been sensitive and responsive to sexual odors. Doty's review (1985) covers axillary odor, hand odor, breath, vaginal, and breast odors. In his 1985 paper, he also discussed the use of fish and plant odors that have been used as aphrodisiacs, in varied cultures, because of similarities to the smell of semen or vaginal odors.

It should also be obvious that sexual arousal alters our perception and interpretation of what we smell. Although, according to Doty, et al (1985) women surpass men in their odor sensitivity by a factor of 35% when identifying odors in both forced choice and free recall test situations. This discrimination is seen in both pre-pubertal and post-pubertal ages (Doty, 1985). Doty felt that this sex difference suggests that humans may have the potential to communicate sexually via smell. New work has shown that sex differences may begin at an early age, and girl babies in contrast to boys, respond as early as three to five months. Doty's review (1985) covers his own work and the literature regarding axillary, hand, vaginal, breast, and breath odors. Of interest, Doty (1975) found that odors developed by women are perceived as more pleasant outside menstrual and luteal, post-ovulatory phases of the menstrual cycle. Human and all mammalian vaginal secretions contain both volatile and non-volatile copulins and pheromones. Gas chromatographic and mass spectrometry analytic tools suggest that there are two types of fatty acid secretions produced by women. As expected, there are qualitative changes that differ between sexually aroused women subjects (Doty, 1985). What these differences mean in relation to male behavioral responses deserves exploration and is a focus of this book.

The language of sexual odors

Pheromones, or sexual odors, constitute an olfactory language. This is based on their chemical components that include steroids or sex hormones; amines and indoles, which are related to proteins and amino acids; and fatty acids, as seen in rancid butter and sour milk. Once released, alone or in mixtures, these substances provide a subconscious communicating system. Rapidly changing olfactory signals provide a script of specific meaning to the recipient. Although, as recipients of these odor stimuli, we most often respond to them without being conscious of their direct influence. Instead, we may find ourselves suddenly feeling relaxed or smiling more broadly and flirting with a new friend, or alternately, suddenly put off by a neighbor who may not be unpleasant, but we are unable to shake off a feeling of irritation or mistrust of them based on odor. As many of the odors we produce are influenced by diet, it is possible that racial, religious, or national affinities or rivalries can be influenced by how one perceives the smell of someone else as related to diet. When we are not certain of something or someone, we often think to ourselves, "Something's fishy here!"

As discussed earlier, Wiener, a pyschopharmacologist, labeled our response to this olfactory language, "the olfactory subconscious," and pointed out that "We shortchange ourselves by comparing the olfactory powers of animals with our own conscious sense of smell while ignoring our olfactory subconscious." In effect, you don't have to rationally define the presence of odor to be influenced by it. The idea of chemical messages passing between me and thee, without either of us being aware of them, may seem startling at first. For this reason, it is good to remember that a number of other improbable sounding channels of vertebrate communication have recently been discovered or confirmed. These range from high to low frequency sounds, and to both the ultraviolet or infrared light spectrums. In support of our position, developmentally, odor awareness begins early in the life of humans; odors are perceived within the first neonatal day (Lipsett, 1963) or certainly the first week of life (Fusari & Pardelli, 1962).

Russell (1976) showed that human infants can respond selectively to their own mother's milk when presented with a choice. In bonding, at two days postpartum, mothers can differentiate the t-shirts of their own babies from those of other infants. Apart from mothers, 80% of adults tested can recognize t-shirt odors of different individuals of different ethnic and racial backgrounds.

Response of newborns to their mother's odors, within the first four days of life can be measured objectively by their increased respiratory and motor response (Lipsett, 1963). This response has survival value as it relates to an infant's ability to recognize and find its mother's nipple. Neonatal sensitivity to odor has been confirmed in a number of other studies and is discussed in an excellent review by Russell (1982) and by Cherfas (1985) who elaborate on Schaael and Porter's work defining infant and maternal odor sensitivity.

That the above can reflect on inborn sex differences is seen in that, Schmidt (1990) has reported that at the age of three to five months, girl babies show a distinct interest in playing with odor-scented rattles, in contrast to boy babies, who are uninterested in odor at that age. However, odor sensitivity in humans declines with age. In fact, one of the biomarkers for the onset of Alzheimer's disease is the loss of odor discrimination.

The question is, why is the above so pertinent? Immature animals have an exaggerated rate of forgetting over a long interval compared to mature animals, but even rodents have the capacity to remember their past. In rodent studies, odor clues from the home environment (smell of siblings, home, nest shavings) affect the character of memory retrieval (Solheim, et al., 1980). Memory is a factor governing brain nuclei, such as the hippocampus, the area of the brain that helps us to remember names and find our way home.

As an example of the importance of odor in childhood, in three- to five-year-olds, it was found that odor preference essentially paralleled that in adults. An exception that has sexual significance was the response to androstenol, or "boar scent," a sex hormone and pheromone found in pigs and human sweat that all the children found unpleasant. However, by adulthood, 50% of one population cannot smell androstenol; of those that can smell it, most males find its smell similar to a "locker room," while most women find it to be pleasant. Unlike Freudian explanations governing Oedipal or Electra fantasies, do we respond to androstenol's smell depending on our inborn love maps governing our predetermined sexual identity? "Pungent" and "rancid" are subjectively negative criteria in attitudes toward odor. This describes locker room odors.

Monerieff (1966) claimed that children below the age of five are not hostile to synthetic smells mimicking human sweat or feces. He said that it takes societal attitudes to turn us away from certain smells. This is now felt to be incorrect as Russell has shown that three- to five-year-old children express the same opinions as to odor preferences as adults.

Negative attitudes towards perspiration are strongly influenced by the advertising industry. While one cannot argue that certain smells, such as those from halitosis or flatulence are unpleasant, not all odors produced by the body are disagreeable and with intimacy, we learn to tolerate each other's odors, pleasant or unpleasant. Mild underarm odor may provide pheromonal stimuli,, while at an intense level of the locker room or laundry hamper, they are repellent.

Television's pervasive commercials to promote a wide variety of vaginal douches tell us that the vagina is a major source of unwanted odor. But, we should be aware that in using such deodorants regularly, we may at the same time be dampening down our sexual identity through sexual odor repression. Without the influence of pheromones, we feel that we might have trouble attracting each other for sexual reproduction to occur.

As an example of the general subtlety of odor awareness, in a clinical experiment, students were asked to identify unfamiliar odors (Cain, 1982; Kirk-Smith, et al, 1983). On first trial, exposed to unfamiliar smells there was a paucity of odor awareness, but on being exposed to the same odor after one week, there was significant improvement in odor response, even though verbal description of the odor was lacking. On multiple exposure, the subject was able to say, "that's like what I smelled last week," even though no odor was identified by the subject the week before. Thus, there may be distinct differences between recognition and detection thresholds (Doty, 1976) for odor awareness.

In many ways the action of pheromones affect our subconscious so our awareness is effected by social and religious attitudes that affect our responses to libido, to our sexual need for each other. For this reason, we react to our loved ones rationally, while we are really responding to them largely at an unconscious, emotional level.

Sexual odors

The human olfactory system is capable of recognizing hundreds of thousands of smells, a skill that professional perfumers and wine tasters rely on for their livelihood. "Noses," as they are called, can distinguish the ingredients of two to three thousand perfume blends. Stoddard has shown that our sensitivity to volatile odors can be surprisingly more acute than that found in rats. The average person is able to distinguish by odor more than 4, 000 chemicals that readily evaporate in the air, including alcohol and acetone. As discussed earlier, an example of how our olfactory sensitivity operates at a molecular level, again, consider how we use hydrogen sulfide, a smelly volatile chemical, to mark cooking gas in order to protect ourselves from asphyxiation or explosion by allowing us to detect the ordinary odor-free gas emitted by our stoves or gas fired furnaces.

Lovers loving

Although in most contemporary pornographic writing, including the frank public confessions and pictorials of oral sex, such as found in the magazine, Penthouse, sexual odor is hardly mentioned as a motivating force. However, if one is aware of the sexual role of odors, pheromones, and copulins are demonstrably present in our erotic literature and have anticipated our scientific speculations in the search for the central focus of human love and lust, which is presented in Chapter III.

During the Elizabethan period in England the power of body odors as sexual stimulants was brought into full play. In Shakespeare's heyday, women unblushingly held peeled apples under their arms until the fruit became permeated with their scent, then offered these "love apples" to their lovers to inhale. It is worth noting that even today in certain parts of Greece and elsewhere in the Balkans, some men carry their handkerchiefs under their arms during festivals and offer them to the women they invite to dance with "highly satisfactory results".

We do not know whether the young maiden he married when he was just sixteen years old gave Edmund Spenser, the greatest of Elizabethan poets, a "love apple." We do know, however, that he was aware of the power of scent as seen in this segment from his magnum opus, *The Faerie Queen.*

In a fresh fountaine, farre from all men's vew,
She bath'd her brest, the boyling heat t'allay;
She bath'd with roses red, and violets blew,
And all the sweetest flowres, that in the forest grew.
The sunne-beames upon her body play'd,
Being through former bathing mollifide,
And pierst unto her wombe, where they embayd
With so sweet sence and secret power unspide,
That in her pregnant flesh they shortly fructified.

Closer to our own time, the 19th century poet Charles Baudelaire had no reservations about proclaiming that lovers are drawn together by their scents. In one of his verses, "Pêrfum Exotique," Baudelaire says that even with his eyes closed, his nostrils sense the warm odor emanating from his lover's breast.

Quand, les deux yeux fermés,	When, with both eyes closed,
en un soir chaud d'automne	on a warm autumn evening
Je respire l'odeur	I inhale the fragrance
de ton sein chaleureux	of your warm bosom.

And no American poet extolled the sensuous qualities of odor as well or as often as Walt Whitman, whose philosophy of sexuality was delineated throughout his *chef d'oevre*, "A Song of Myself," which was a century ahead of his time. Whitman intuited the presence of pheromones in our lives in numerous passages of rapturous self-elation:

Houses and rooms are full of perfumes, the shelves are crowded with perfumes,
I breathe the fragrance myself and know it and like it
The distillation would intoxicate me also, but I shall not let it

The description of sexual odors by novelists is so numerous that one could fill a fair-sized volume with excerpts. For example, Joseph Heller, in *God Knows*, reconstructs a delightfully irreverent account of the life and times of the Old Testament's King David. In Heller's narrative, King David is dying and when the voluptuous Abishag is brought to his chambers to keep him warm and perhaps revive his once legendary libido, the elderly regent muses:

"I wonder if she is old enough to know how majestic and virile I used to be before my muscles wasted and I began to wither with age. Beneath the lotions with which she freshens herself I can smell the coarse magnetic secretions of the natural human woman, and I want her."

Anais Nin, an American writer of Spanish and French descent, was virtually unknown as a writer for most of her life. However, with the publication in 1965 of her correspondence with Henry Miller and in the following year the first of what would become her six volume *Diary*, she drew a great deal of attention. These literary journals revealed a vital and profoundly gifted woman who had lived a varied and complex sexual life. One has only to read her diary entries about Henry Miller during the tempestuous years of their *l'affaire d'amour* to recognize the importance that smell played in their sexual foreplay. In one journal entry, she wrote:

"His kisses are wet like rain. I have swallowed his sperm and he has kissed the sperm off my lips. I have smelled my own honey on his mouth."

During a brief period she was in love with both Miller and his wife, June, and extolled this bisexual arrangement. As for the powerful sway of odors, here is what she wrote in one of her journal entries, this one referring to her husband, Hugh Guiler, she wrote:

"While I was away, he found my black lace underwear, kissed it, found the odor of me, and inhaled it with such joy."

In one of her stories, Nin portrays a man whose attraction to his chosen woman is heightened by "the odor of her sex—pungent shell and sea odors, as if women came out of the sea as Venus did." What Anais Nin was describing, both in her journals and letters as well as the short stories just cited undoubtedly shocked some readers, while titillating others; certainly most readers regarded her observations as quasi-pornography. Today, however, after the extensive research on sex by Kinsey, Masters, and Johnson, and others, and the ready availability of pornography, we should not be shocked by Nin's exploration of her sexuality.

Regarding the importance of sexual odors we welcome the insights of Dr. Helen E. Fisher, an anthropologist associated with the American Museum of Natural History, in her splendid book, *Anatomy of Love*, (W.W. Norton, 1992):

"When you meet someone new whom you find attractive, you probably like the smell of him, and this helps predispose you to romance. Then, once infatuation flowers, the scent of your sweetheart becomes an aphrodisiac, a continuing stimulant in the love affair."

In literature the descriptions of pheromonal interplay in sexual matters are not restricted solely to fiction. Pioneer sexologist, Havelock Ellis, relays a story about a certain Asiatic prince who often had his harem wives race in the seraglio garden until they were perspiring heavily. Afterwards, he would request that their sweat-soaked garments be brought to him and he would select his consort for the evening solely by her odor.

There is also the well-known anecdote relating to Napoleon Bonaparte's affinity for sexual odors. His biographers cite a letter Napoleon sent to his inamorata, Josephine, in which he wrote, "I will be arriving in Paris tomorrow evening. Don't wash."

The late 19th century chronicler of Parisian decadence, Jori Karl Huysman, was said to openly follow women through the fields, smelling them. His contemporary Flaubert was not insensitive to odors, either. In a letter to one of the women in his life, he wrote, "In daydreams, I live in the folds of your dress, in the fine curls of your hair. I have some of these here—how good they smell." And even the poet Goethe once confessed that, on a two-day trip away from his lady friend, he took her bodice with him in order to have available the scent of her body.

One American chronicler of contemporary sexual practices, Nancy Friday, has been very successful in persuading "average" people to record their erotic practices and fantasies and send them to her. Her first book, *My Secret Garden*, has already gone through 29 printings. In subsequent books, *Men in Love* and *Forbidden Flowers*, she offers many stories culled from letters she received from both men and women. These frank, earthy accounts, to be sure, have no major literary value – and although such casual reports about sexuality are notoriously unreliable, these are from Americans of all walks of life and they reveal the wide range of sexual fantasies and practices in our country that deal with scent.

Diane Ackerman in her delightful book, *A Natural History of the Senses* points out that Helen Keller had a "miraculous gift for deciphering the fragrant palimpsest of life that most of us read as a blur." That Keller's sensuality was grounded in smell can readily be seen in the following passage from her writings:

"Masculine exhalations are, as a rule, stronger, more vivid, more widely differentiated than those of women. In the odor of young men there is something elemental, as of fire, storm, and salt sea. It pulsates with buoyancy and desire. It suggests all the things strong and beautiful and joyous and gives me a sense of physical happiness."

As this brief survey indicates, the intoxicating potential of sexual odor to attract and tantalize us in romantic interludes has been recorded in legend, myth, poem, song, and story after story. All reveal the timeless dance between lovers that is often orchestrated by the provocative lure of sexual odors.

To see it published upsets our religious strictures, yet over $10 billion is spent on salacious films and many of us may be involved in the search for pornography. If what those searching for pornography seek is visual in its attraction, what would happen if it also included a sensory appeal to our vomeronasal receptors?

With apologies to the prudish:
"All these combined into an elixir of lust . . . a cantharides of passion . . . nostrils dilated voluptuously as he quaffed the perfume, that blend of erotic titillation. And for her . . . her delicate nostrils dilated as she, in turn, was impregnated with the semen scent of his tool, with the male aroma of his semen-laden testicles . . . the intimate aroma of his privates, and for her, it was a new, singularly stirring perfume." (Anonymous, *The Master*, Pendulum Books, Atlanta, 1963).

From the French pornographic novel:
"What is better than to plunge one's nose or mouth into a moist vagina? To feel under one's tongue the texture of lips, to take them completely in your

mouth, to fondle them, while the odor of the sea fills your nostrils – to make the pearl of the clitoris harden, to aspire it – to extend the point of the tongue into the moisture of the vagina . . ."
(Claudio Verdi, Memoires D'un Observe, Media 1000, Paris)

Finally, to avoid, only a masculine focus, another striking example is found in *There She Blows*, (Anonymous, Pendulum Books, Atlanta, 1968). Here we have the sexual biography of a jazz musician of the 1930s whose uninhibited lover speaks frankly about the oral focus of her sexuality:

"Hope kept my **** in her mouth and I jerked her off until the bus began to slow down for the next stop and then she sat up and pulled her skirt down. 'Wipe your mouth off, it looks juicy,' I said. She did . . . 'My mouth gets that way when I smell oranges. Everybody sees that slobber when I go down on them or when I'm thinking about going down on them, and sometimes it isn't that at all. If there are oranges anywhere in the room, my mouth does that. Isn't that funny?' she said. "It just looked a little wet,' I said. 'Does your cunt get wet when you smell oranges?'

'No, but it gets wet when I smell prick. It honestly does and, if I am going down on a man, when I get my nose near his cock, I can feel myself begin to pour inside.'

'I don't French so much when I am sober as when I am tight. When I get tight I want to spend all my time on my knees with a cock shoved into my face. I shouldn't tell you this."

This pornographic book expands its story to involve its female protagonist in bisexual exchanges with the same emphasis on odor as the factor influencing cunnilingus as it did in her previous enthusiasm for fellatio. In this particular explicit novel, oral sex is not a degrading compulsion, or based on the forced aggression of a dominant controlling male. The women who indulge their odor-mediated fantasies in this novel are not passive vehicles for the submissive satisfaction of men, nor are they sadomasochistically compelled to act in this manner. Instead, if there is any truth to this experience, we have among the first novelistic expressions of a dominating pheromonal response in women that provides what might be vomeronasal underpinnings of a woman's enthusiasm for oral sex. Is this true?

While all the above is possible and probably true, one must establish acts of oral sex in relation to its mammalian background where pheromonal action stimulates a response that is not unlike passionate kissing for which we have no rational explanation. Are mammals other than man involved in genital kissing? Of course they do! Is fellatio stimulated by the generation of genital odor or is it the result of an attempt at reciprocity, an exchange of pleasure? Finally, how often is this the end result of male intimidation of the weaker sex forcing them to surrender to power? To threaten, or to acceptance of an alternative that is not as intimidating as intercourse itself.

Why has the above become popular with 50% of adolescents? Does it relate to the behavior of our ex-President who did not consider it the equivalent of sexual intercourse?

In conclusion, perhaps the best contemporary demonstration of pheromones in action is found in Neil Simon's play, *The Star Spangled Girl*, 1970-1971, which presents a delightful view of love and infatuation and how smell can play a delicious part in this dance!

Andy: Who's that, Norman?

Norman: Never mind who it is, I saw her first.

Andy: All right, you saw her first. Who is she?

Norman (turns front): Her name is Sophie Rauschmeyer and she just moved into the empty apartment next door and she just gave me a fruit cake with rum in it and I love her. (Running left, right, and all over the room) Wahoo! Did you see what moved into this building? Next door to where I live! It's for me. All for me. God loves me and He gave me something wonderful.

Andy: (Happy for Norman, on the bottom step) I was going to get you one for Christmas.

Norman: (He is now dancing all over the room) Did you smell her? Did you get one whiff of that fragrance? Did you open your entire nose and smell that girl?

Andy: (Comes down onto the stage floor and goes stage left) I was upstairs, she didn't smell that far. . .I need your dancing shoes.

Norman: Didn't smell that far? It's all over the room. It's even out in the hall. I'll bet she's inundated the whole lousy neighborhood. They're gonna start raising rents. And you stay away from her.

Andy: What are you going to do?

Norman: Get a hold of myself? Are you kidding? My functioning days are over. I've become an animal. I've developed senses no man has ever used before. I can smell the shampoo in her hair three city blocks away. I can have my radio turned up full blast and still hear her taking off her stockings! Don't you understand, *she turns me on!* From my head to my toes, I take one look at her and I light up. This month alone my personal electric bill will be over two hundred dollars..."

As the play develops, Norman is no longer in love with Sophie. He no longer is aware of her smell and instead, Andy falls in love with Sophie and the play ends happily with Andy and Sophie smelling each other. Neil Simon has presented us with a pheromonal vision of what love is, in a contemporary setting for our time. In the next chapter, we will learn more about the physiological "wiring" behind sexual attraction and how this draws lovers together and helps establish all of our intimate relationships.

Spiritual sex practices of Tantric Buddhism

In the search for religious acceptance of oral sexuality, one must look away from our Judeo-Christian or Moslem morality. It is perhaps in the tradition of Buddhism distinct from its focus on celibacy that one can find a teaching that welcomes a "passionate enlightenment" that permits sexual practices divorced from reproduction. What tantric practice emphasizes is that the energies awakened by sexual union can be transformed into very refined states of consciousness. "There is a tantric teaching to the effect that without the practice of sexual union and without integrating one's energies at that level, it is impossible to attain enlightenment." What is said is that men are to worship women, that they should "take refuge in the vulva of an esteemed woman" and should even "be willing to touch and ingest every substance discharged by a woman's body."

Tantric philosophy views every woman who employs its practices as a goddess and equally high esteem is bestowed upon the men who serve the goddess. Sexuality is seen as an affirmation and celebration of divinity in the Universe and within each Individual. It permits us to utilize passion and sexual energy as a key to enlightenment. "The intimate offering of sexual pleasure is appropriately called the "secret offering" that proceeds in stages. "One of the goals of erotic play is to stimulate the flow of the woman's sexual fluid . . . the tip of the phallus distills nectar from the corolla of the woman's lotus – tantric union requires a mixing of sexual fluids, for the purpose of spiritual illumination rather than procreation.

"The tantric pattern, in which the female fluids are deliberately absorbed by the male is a reversal of ordinary conjugal union, in which it is primarily the woman who absorbs the male fluid." It seems that in tantric ritual, this esoteric, private form of Buddhism that the exchange of genital fluid is the mutual responsibility of both partners.

Here we should pause to reflect on what cunnilingus and fellatio represent for those that are involved. Does it represent an aesthetic far removed from reciprocal pleasure or coercion that permits the mind to escape its boundaries in order to:

> *"Inhale scents*
> *Taste delicious flowers*
> *Feel textures*
> *Use the objects of the five senses to quickly attain supreme Buddhahood"*

Orgasm

In humans, the situation is a more subtle one, but, as an example where oral sex may play a role in humans' sperm "flowback," its vaginal return may reverse the loss of 35% of injected sperm, but this number decreases if a woman's orgasms take place soon after the man's ejaculation. Orgasm is associated with the contraction of the walls of the outer third of the vagina. This decreases flowback, which is also associated with temporary coagulation of the ejaculate. Intromission is not a guarantee of fertilization. The act of oral sex leading to orgasm may provide a successful path to orgasm enhancing a woman's pleasure, bonding, and the subsequent pregnancy.

Cryptic choice

The thrusting movements of the male are not the only route to our species propagation or to a woman's heart. In similar fashion, the same may be true to a woman's place in satisfying the man. The answer is not seen in sex as sport, where success is measured by the cryptic female choice.

Eberhard has written a text dealing with a females "cryptic" or hidden control of her fertility. This relates to her successful choice of mates resulting in intromission and the production of offspring. It is often the decision of the female that in evolution determines a fertile outcome to copulation. In his review, Eberhard demonstrates the importance of female choice throughout the animal kingdom, ranging from insects to spiders, crustacea, birds, and mammals.

Adaptations that effect female selection of mates are protean in their variation. Those that reflect on pheromonal action in mammals are varied. For example, female lab mice respond differently to male hormones depending on age. Pre-pubertal females avoid the male smell, while adult females are attracted to it. A strange male smell to a pregnant female can result in abortion (in what is known as the Bruce effect), resulting in her becoming responsive to the new male who thus gains a genetic advantage.

Frequency of intercourse relates to mutual satisfaction that must be seen in both pre- and post-copulatory behavior. Of interest, Eberhard describes the behavior of an African antelope, the Uganda kub, where the male, post copulatory, stimulates the female by stroking her with its forelegs and by licking her genitals. Why does he do it? This action enhances the movement of his sperm to achieve successful fertilization. In human terms, why should we consider post-coital interaction when pleasure, reproduction, or reassurance as to commitment transcends sleep induction beyond satiation.

It is our feeling that oral sex, governed by pheromones, is not only an act of bonding that explains pheromonal interaction, but that it may also have a place in contributing to a successful pregnancy and parental commitment toward that result.

Chapter 3

We will find thy love more fragrant than wine.
— King Solomon

Until recently, our ability to detect and respond to sexual odors was customarily denied in polite society. While we do not have difficulty in savoring the smell of a freshly baked apple pie, we are apt to politely avoid discussion of how wonderfully tantalizing our lover's clothes smell, or similarly, how comforting a loved one's sweater is to us in his or her absence. Despite the sexual revolution in our own time, we are only just becoming aware of the importance of sexual odors in our lives.

The mythology of love

"We can safely say, therefore, that whereas some moralists may find it possible to make a distinction between two spheres and reigns – one of flesh, the other of spirit, one of time, the other of eternity – wherever love arises such definitions vanish, and a sense of life awakens in which all such oppositions are one."

— Joseph Campbell

Joseph Campbell, in his "Myths to Live By," outlines the major conflict that exists between eros and the spiritual order of love. The opposite of eros is lust or "animal passion." This is seen best in the work of the 12th and 13th century troubadours, or the minnesingers who viewed love as "amour." "Amour" as expressing the passion of that time, was personal and discriminative. It was born in the "eyes and the heart." Those specifically entranced by this experience were drawn to a specific individual and the feelings involved were of "bitter sweetness and dear grief." In the middle ages, it was a love that could not be fully consummated between couples because of the sanctity of chastity and the immediate physical threat of corporal punishment or that of eternal damnation for violating God's laws related to adultery. It must be remembered that marriage during that period was a business or family arrangement, and "amor" could not break the sacrament of marriage without punishment. You thus had courtly love, where poetry and deeds had to substitute for physicality.

The amor of the troubadours, and that of our current day, while governed by sight or vision of the loved one, is, we feel, made even more specific and everlasting by the pheromones that strengthened the image of our loved ones. A knight going into battle with the scarf of his lady could have been inspired to fight in her honor, by the odor clinging to the scarf. The mystical attraction in the legends of Tristan and Isolde, which speak of "poisoned drink," casting the spell of attraction between the lovers might be based less romantically on physiologic reality induced by pheromonal affinity that activates the olfactory receptors of our brain. To paraphrase Campbell, whether this attraction produces a heaven or a hell, is not as important as the fact that the affinity puts "you in your proper place, which is exactly where you want to be." This "proper place" put the lovers in close affinity to their olfactory "love maps," which, if not for eternity, at least for a time, holds us together.

Possession, penetration, and satiation

For some men, the modus operandi for their sexual seduction is summarized in the saying, "Wham, bam, thank you ma'am!" For some men this has been the key to their persona in interacting with woman. In that regard, Andrea Dworkin (*Intercourse*, Free Press, 1987) may not have been wrong ascribing male expressions of love to a focus on male penetration followed by satiation; intercourse governed by lust. However, will that change? Will awareness of the pheromonal connection provide women with the tenderness from their partners that can become part of a mutually satisfying sexuality? Holding, touching, kissing, licking, so that our mutual sebaceous secretions, our skin, our mouille, provide for us. Will awareness of pheromones help women perceive themselves and be perceived by others as "goddesses?" Women do not need to define themselves strictly as mothers and wives as proscribed by orthodox religious traditions. Can they be perceived as "goddesses" contributing to both mutual pleasure and/or reproduction?

According to Dworkin, "Intercourse remains a means . . . of physiologically making a woman inferior: communicating to her . . . her own inferior status, impressing it on her, burning it into her by shoving it into her, over and over, pushing and thrusting until she gives up and gives in . . . which is called 'surrender' in the male lexicon." These statements could easily be categorized as "male bashing" were it not for the fact that the need to subdue male aggression has been previously noted in anthropological studies. Will the awareness of pheromones, beyond the male stimulus provided by Viagara, provide an opportunity to diffuse the aggressive male by teaching him to share behavior governed by the release of pheromones by the one we love?

In addition, how many of us are aware of the medical and social problems associated with male access to Viagra? An erection, which provides male satisfaction, can constitute a rapine invasion in a woman who is not prepared by tenderness, pheromones and oral and physical caressing.

This issue is both physiologic and cultural as many of the world's religions or social structures see women as second-class citizens who are a threat to male morality because of pheromonal generation or its equivalent. The contrast is extreme: purdah, the floor-length gowns and veils worn by Moslem women, as compared to bikinis. Or, equally extreme to the above contrast is seen in clitorectomy versus genitalia pierced with jewelry as societal practice.

Fundamentalists insist that the purpose of humans is to reproduce and populate the world. What they fail to see is that without the influence of pheromones, we could not be able to attract each other for sexual reproduction and the formation of long-term familial bonds.

Mammalian pheromone behavior: rodents
Human sexual behavior, to be completely understood, must be seen in comparison with animal behavior. While it is obvious that vision is a key element in adult sexual contacts, the relation of odor to our sexual behavior has been largely ignored despite its prominent role throughout the animal kingdom. This is particularly true of sex related odor influences in the developing child. This chapter gives us a short review of mammalian responses to odor in a sexual content.

Vomeronasal functional presence in mammals is associated with a characteristic sniffing sexual behavior in males ("flehman") seen in ruminants, elephants, carnivores, New World monkeys (Epple, 1985) and other mammals as part of the male response to estrus-induced vaginal odors (Wysocki, 1979).

From clinical experience and in discussion with others, when interviewed, those who practice oral sex, perform a ritual similar to flehman found in horses and other mammals. Sexual sniffing is not unknown in humans and Margaret Johns, in an excellent review (1985) postulates that it may be important to human sexual responses.

Flehman can also be seen in many non-human primates (Epple, 1985) and it is our contention that cunnilingus and fellatio may be based on similar responses in humans. Sexual sniffing, intrinsic to human behavior, is seen when we take advantage of the residual pheromonal qualities of our sexual secretions which affect us, not only in the search for reciprocal pleasure, but as an act important to bonding between couples that goes beyond copulation as its single goal, but introduces socialization as an aspect of odor interaction.

With mice, olfactory thresholds are governed by their sexual state. The most sensitive olfactory thresholds are to n-butyric acid, a vaginal product. Electrical olfactory bulb recordings in the brain that respond to this pheromone during estrus and the period of highest female stimulated sexual activity have determined this. There is a seven-fold rise of threshold of detection of odorant molecules (Schmidt, 1978) during this period. This shows the relationship of hormonal influences to odor detection. As discussed previously, butyric acid is also found in human vaginal secretions, as well as in rancid milk.

Of importance to socialization in our understanding of human behavior, in mice, male hormones that influence social dominance govern aggression. A high level of testosterone, the male hormone, triggers an odor release in the commanding male that maintains his dominance over the rest of the group. Young male mice exposed to pooled urine from either dominant or subordinate adult mice spend more time sniffing the urine of subordinate mice. They can clearly detect an odor difference between dominant and subordinate males. (Hennessey, 1980)

Sexual selectivity in male mice is affected by their early exposure to the odor of their mother. In social development, mammals are known to be affected by early odor exposure. Olfactory clues govern filial responsiveness in rats, i.e., nipple and head orientation to the mother. As another example, nursing female mice scented with verbena (lemon scent) alters the mature response of their male offspring; at sexual maturity, these males raised with a lemon-scented mother preferred mating with females similarly scented. In contrast, mice raised with natural odors prefer normally scented, estrus females.

In male mice whose parents were coated with violet scent, again, after scent conditioning, normal sexual odors did not exert the same effect on sexual preference. Rather, the preference was directed to the odor of violet in estrus females (Mainardi et al, 1965). Similar effects have been described for citral scented rats (Fillion and Blass, 1986).

In guinea pigs, male sexual behavior in relation to the speed of sexual involvement with an estrous female: latency to mount, mounting and sex drive, showed increased responsiveness in the presence of their familial rearing odors (Carter, 1972; Yamazaki, 1979; Boyse, 1983). This remarkable discriminatory sensitivity is the key to social and sexual preference (Jones and Partridge, 1983).

A mouse has no trouble determining its genealogy; mice can tell their Virginian cousins from their North Carolinian ones. In human terms, this degree of odor discrimination would be an aid to snobbery. If we had the same degree of sensitivity as mice, one could determine membership in an exclusive country club based on the smell of one's urine.

What this suggests is that we are identified as distinct individuals by our smell, and that our odor has a family-related distinction based on genetics independent of the diet consumed. The way our relatives smell is different from the way our friends or strangers smell.

In contrast to observations, where odor familiarization stimulates sexual preference, Money (1986) discussed the behavior of the prairie vole (Getz, 1981). This rodent requires the introduction of a strange male to induce female sexual behavior. Virgin females are reproductively dormant as long as they continue to live with familiar male relatives. On nasogenital grooming, i.e., sniffing and licking of the genitals of a female by a strange male, estrus occurs within two days and monogamous pair bonding develops involving the non-familiar male.

In contrast to voles, Syrian and Turkish male hamsters show a strong preference for a close female family member over females that are not related. Foster rearing modifies the preference, but does not eliminate it. This phenomenon is clearly an odor preference based on vomeronasal function (Murphy, 1980).

In further support for odor conditioning responses, Nyby (1978), in an excellent review, have presented evidence in varied species ranging from house mice to dogs and deer where certain infant and adult encounters are necessary for natural odors (familial) or foreign odors to be preferred or avoided. These odors condition behavior. Fillion and Blass have repeated this in 1986, in rats.

Perfuming sexually available female rats for their first heterosexual encounter conditions adult male rats to react vocally to the artificial perfume odor in similar fashion to their response to female urine (Nyby, 1978). The female urine stimulus is lost unless reinforced by an active female sexual response (Dizinno, 1978) that permits mounting.

A secretory odor in hamster pups was governed by their male hormone testosterone levels (Johnson & Codlin, 1979). The female hormone, estrogen, is a factor in male response to females. As an example, experienced male rats were not attracted to females following surgical loss of their pituitary glands, which concomitant loss of estrogenic capacity.

Another female hormone, progesterone, given in the same rat model decreases sexual attractiveness (Thody, 1981). Progesterone is produced during the post-ovulatory period in women, during the two-week period prior to menstruation, or during pregnancy. Progesterone is used with estrogen in birth control. Does it have any affect on human pheromonal attractiveness?

Of interest to vaginal pheromonal effects, both the hamster (Singer, 1976) and rat (Gawienoski & Stacewicz-Sapuntzakis, 1978), is attracted to sulfur-containing compounds which are among the volatiles also given off by the human body (Ellin, 1974.)

The urine of mature male rodents accelerates puberty in females, while female urine (Drickamer, 1977) exposure delays puberty. In rats, the sex-stimulating female must be new to the male (Tiepir, 1965). In a two choice odor preference test, male rats prefer a strange female to the odor of a previously monogamous mate. The female, in contrast, preferred the odor of the male with which she was monogamously coupled (Carr, 1980). Male rats may be behaving more like the stereotype of their male human counterparts.

In relation to pheromonal odor similarities between rodents and humans, during the menstrual cycle, there is a difference in olfactory sensitivity to exatolide (pentadecanolide), a perfume fixative with a musk-like odor (Vierline & Rock, 1967). This is similar to what has been seen for exatolide in female mice relevant to electrical recording of olfactory bulb sensitivity during ovulation (Schmidt, 1978). Le Mangen (1952) found that adult women were sensitive to exatolide while young children and adult men could barely detect it, and 50% of men could not smell it at all. This is one of the most striking distinctive sexual difference between men and women in odor awareness. This obviously is important to the perfume industry, as in designing perfumes attractive to men or women, such differences have to be kept in mind.

In support of the above, in rats, a relationship has been found between olfaction and the locus coeruleus and the dorsal raphe nucleus of the brain. These are special areas of the brain that govern vigilance states and social behavior (Cattarelli & Chanel, 1979). The pattern of behavior elicited by odor varies with the odor introduced; "group rat odor" eliciting a locomotion response sniffing and rearing while "fox odor" elicits a freezing behavior. These are instinctive responses and although responses of this kind are not readily visible as part of human behavior: we must look for them, as we have the neural organization and responding systems that are not much different than those seen in rats and other mammals.

Apart from it's value in searching for food, odor detection is critical to species survival as it is essential for animal sexual reproduction, in humans, as well as in rodents. Of interest, olfactory neurons regenerate in cyclical fashion in mammals that suggests the importance of smell to human development and behavior. Throughout the life of vertebrates replacement of olfactory neurons occurs. No other neural system in mammals has this degree of regenerative capacity.

Nipple attachment in newborn rats is stimulated by amniotic fluid derived from the fluid that suspends them in utero, as well as maternal saliva (Teicher & Blass, 1977). Similar stimulating effects produced by amniotic fluid are found in sheep.

In terms of social behavior, rat pups recognize their own nest bedding and prefer it, but by 16 days, they are indifferent to its odor and by 20 days, they prefer strange bedding (Carr, 1979). This, of course, can motivate rat progeny to leave their nest.

Surgical removal of the sense of smell with olfactory bulbectomy aborts aggressive behavior in the male mouse and interferes with female maternal behavior (Neckers, 1975).

The attractiveness of the male rat for the female is based on male hormone odor-related factors. Castrated males do not smell the same to females, but this attraction can be restored by dihydrotestosterone replacement (Drewett & Spiter, 1979), a universal mammalian male hormone determinant.

Aggressive activity between hamster males is reduced when males are covered by vaginal discharge odors obtained from estrus females (Murphy, 1973). Similar behavior is seen in the hamster where vaginal sexual odors adhering to skin and hair affect male copulatory behavior (Murphy, 1973, O'Connell & Meredith, 1984).

Urinary modulating effects via odor may be important to male rodent identity: male mice isolated in groups away from females have lower testosterone and increased production of enzymes that lower male sex hormonal synthesis. These enzymes decrease the availability of testosterone as compared to what is found with rearing in heterosexual company. However, exposure to bedding from females restores normal male hormonal production (Dessi-Fulgheri, 1972) in these isolated males. This has been described earlier by Steinach (1936) and Purvis & Haynes (1978). In the latter case, female urine odor restores testosterone production in male rats previously isolated from females.

In female mice kept under crowded conditions, there is a continuous state of diestrus, estrogen-related (sexual receptivity) induced by the absence of males, which can be normalized by male odors (Sahu & Gosh, 1982). In mice, a whiff of the opposite sex restores physiologic sexual equilibrium. Might the same be true for humans? Recalling aging King David's loss of virility, for recovery, he was brought a seductive Shulamite woman to his bed. Was this an odor stimulus? Women, in a male-dominated society, have not had a similar opportunity. Do Hollywood luminaries like Elizabeth Taylor present an equal case for the odor of a younger male as a rejuvenating force?

Important to our own physiologic usefulness, in view of rodent odor effects on sexual response, one wonders if human sexually induced odors could overcome or delay the hormonal deficiencies of the climacteric or menopause.

Primates

As humans, we resemble apes most closely, and with contemporary techniques we can now establish clinical differences between us primates, apes and monkeys based on DNA affinities. On this basis, we differ from our closest evolutionary relative, the chimpanzee, by only 1.6% of our DNA. In time estimates, the divergence from a common monkey ancestor is approximately seven million years.

The role of sexual odor in monkeys has been widely studied. (Michael, 1969; Michael & Deveang, 1968, 1971; Keveang, 1976.) For example, a male Rhesus monkey, when paired simultaneously with two females, will show a definite preference for one of them. This is determined by ovarian function that produces estrogen, the female hormone. Male preference (Evritt & Herbert, 1969) is governed by estrogen in the female that stimulates her pheromonal production. Thus, ovarian-governed hormonal cycling, which controls the secretory function of vaginal mucosa and sweat glands, stimulates the male Rhesus (Macaca Mulatta) monkey. (Michael, 1972).

Male grooming of female Rhesus monkeys is also conditioned by their ovarian cycle. "Flea-picking" increases proportionately to pheromonal production based on vaginal secretion. Application of estrogenically stimulated vaginal secretions to non-ovulating females makes them attractive to the male Rhesus (Keverne & Michael, 1971).

Copulins

Odor is the critical attractive stimulus for the male. Estrogen produces a more enthusiastic masculine interest when applied vaginally than when given orally or by systemic injection. The anatomic localized presence of enhanced vaginal secretion is more pertinent to stimulating male interest than female behavioral changes. What this means is that the female Rhesus' behavior is less critical to male interest than the quality of her vaginal odor (Michael, 1969). This is confirmed by experiments wherein plugging the nose of the male Rhesus abolished his sexual interest.

What the above implies for us is that the sexual motivation of a woman can be less important to male response at a particular moment than if she is emitting a positive pheromonal signal. As will be discussed, there is a problem if a woman is emitting a discordant pheromonal "message" which can lead to "date rape". As difficult as it may be to consider, date rape may have a physiologic explanation.

As discussed, the product of vaginal fatty acids produced by bacterial action on vaginal secretions have been termed "copulins" because of their affect on sexual behavior (Bonsall & Michael, 1980). Copulins have been found both in the great apes and in humans, but results are variable as to the consistency of their fatty acid composition (Fox, 1979) that varies with menstrual cycle and species. Fox (1982) feels that chimpanzee copulins may act as primer pheromones stimulating male interest and copulatory behavior.

Kirk-Smith (1978) studied the effects of androstenol and/or aliphatic volatile acid mixtures (copulins) found in the primate vagina. They placed these pheromones on surgical masks to study the effects of these sexual odors on evaluation of human candidates interviewed for a specific job. The exposure effect was confined to the assessment of male student candidates by female raters. Those tested were unaware of the odor impregnation of the facemasks, but were told the facemasks were worn to conceal facial expression from the interviewer during the test evaluation. Adrostenol enhanced favorable ratings, while copulin fatty acid products had the opposite effect.

Marking

In excellent reviews, Epple (1974) Epple and Smith (1985) discuss olfactory communication in South American New World primates. Apart from pheromonal sexual arousal odors, they discuss "partner marking." In marmosets "partner marking" enhances pair bonding in these species. The males mark their partners by rubbing their circumgenital pelvic glands against their chosen female. This is a socially bonding act that is separate from sexual intercourse itself.

In humans, mutual pelvic contact, "frottage," or the "dry hump," as is seen in alternatives to intercourse, may also be seen as an atavistic primate marking gesture. While men and women have rubbed their pelvises together on countless dance floors or hallways, we usually see this as a preliminary to intercourse or as a frustrated substitute for it. However, it may also represent an atavistic mark of possession.

Again, pregnant female marmosets produce genital odors that are particularly attractive to their mates. Epple and Smith speculate that this may have survival value in preparing the male to participate in rearing, and/or to diminish male aggression to the newborn.

As in the other mammals, urine is a prime marking factor in monkeys. In spider monkeys (aeteles), for example, males are highly motivated to sample female odors during all stages of the reproductive cycle. Stimulated by female odors, the males manipulate the large clitoris of the females, sniffing their hands after they do so in a variety of social circumstances. Similar behavior has been reported for chimpanzees (Nishida, 1970) wherein females are attracted to the odor of male genitalia.

Foreplay
Our human interest in the genitalia of our partners has always been assumed to relate to the need to reciprocally stimulate one another to achieve acceptance for the act of copulation. Foreplay, which involves reaching out to one's partner for genital or breast fondling or stroking is traditionally seen as a simple prelude to the more satisfactory sexually shared act of male penetration.

Another way to look at shared genital stimulation is that it produces the arousal resulting in the lubrication that contains the pheromones. These sexual releasers then act, as stimuli for copulation and oral sex. Even without the sex act itself, imbibing sexual odors can be an end unto itself. Some men relive the presence of their loved ones by sniffing their fingers or touching their unwashed genitals that bring the adherent odor to their nose. In this sense, men are like spider monkeys. We re-experience sexual delight in a limerant manner by re-experiencing the odor.

As in other mammals, in Rhesus monkeys, short chain aliphatic acids, pheromones under estrogen control, are sexually stimulatory to the male. At this point it is important again to realize that many of these pheromones generated by simians or other mammals are based upon bacterial breakdown products produced on the skin or by secretions derived particularly from the genital area.

As an example of the effect of natural vaginal odors, is that rhesus males masturbate under the influence of these vaginal pheromones when the female is not available (Michael, 1971).

In monkeys, male and female sexual behavior is distinctly different (Linnankoski, 1981).   Male stump tail monkeys masturbate in the presence of females however, females do not show masturbatory activity. In stump-tails, during copulation, females always turn around to face the males, and do not try to release themselves after male ejaculation. As in humans, salivary exchange is seen on face-to-face contact and the male begins copulation following prior perineal sniffing, fingering, and mounting. Vocalization and lip smacking accompany sexual activity and one female was seen to stimulate her clitoris during male perineal investigation and copulation.

Monkeys require ancillary enhancers for optimal sexual stimulation (Keverne, 1976). With a loss of pheromonal female input male copulatory response and interest decreases, but there may be a period of increased activity which Keverne (1976) feels may be a compensatory effort where tactile stimulation acts as a substitute for the loss of odor stimulation. As in humans, odor is not by itself sufficient to dominate as the prime motivator in all sexual situations.

In most Old World (African or Asian) monkeys, vision is the males' prime signal as to the availability of the female. Her sexual skin becomes tumescent and highly vascular during estrus. While the temperature of the skin is elevated there is no evidence that its hot surface engorged by blood vessels releases more odor-releasing substances. While this is a possibility, in New World monkeys, where odor attraction is clearly predominant, there is the absence of highly visible sexual skin engorgement seen in most African or Asian monkeys, to visually attract the male. An exception are Macaques, Old World monkeys, with little sexual skin and they may compensate with copious vaginal secretions during estrus when they are sexually available.

Vision

Of interest, where highly colored, visual sexual skin is a behavioral factor in bringing the sexes together, we must consider this development possible evidence for the beginning of mammalian color vision that is found in prosimians. Color vision as a key feature of primate development is now thought to be an evolutionary advantage to detecting ripe fruit in food gathering. Thus, the search for food and the search for sex become commingled with the evolutionary onset of color vision.

Although perfume artificially applied or native to women as pheromones may be important, their influence is subtle. As an example of difference, in prosimians and New World monkeys, odor marking is present, in 56% or 75%, while in Old World monkeys who are more dependent on visual attraction, this occurs in only 5% in a large series based on a study of different species.

In a study of the sexual behavior of captive lowland gorillas, Hess describes the palpable odor of the estrus female detectable to any observer. However, a key to female gorilla proceptive interest in the male is the fixed gaze of the female on the male of her choice. Nancy Regan's gaze in admiration of our now ill-retired President is similar to what one sees in estrus female gorillas. We see the same in girls enamored of rock stars. Lovers' eyes have "stars in them," as they gaze at each other.

Estrus

With estrus in gorillas, males are stimulated to touch genitals or armpits of the females and after touching they put their fingers to their mouths or tongue. This occurs in post-copulatory situations as well. Young gorillas in the vicinity of sexual activity try to sample female sexual secretions as well.

The male gorilla, guaranteed his sexual success via his harem monopoly, needs no massive spermatic discharge, and as a consequence, his testicles are almost non-palpable. His females coming into estrus are perceptively cooperative and his penis need not be large to do the job.

In a caged environment, male gorillas have been seen to perform cunnilingus and Fossey, states that in the wild, "at no time during their proximity, were adults seen to touch or sniff one another's genital region, although immature animals of both sexes not infrequently sniffed an estrus females' rump."

Unlike the bonobos (the pigmy chimp) and humans, the sexual position of gorillas is always dorso-ventral in male to female sexual interaction. However, there are reports of female homosexual activity where ventero-ventral intercourse was seen.

Despite differences in reproductive and child-rearing (familial) strategies, both the gibbons and orangutans practice oral sex. Before coitus, this takes place for many minutes as primarily a male prerogative, but both males and females show interest in genital odors, again smelling secretions at their source or on their hands. Similar finger sniffing behavior is seen in gorillas.

Odor plays a role in maternal mother-child bonding in primates. As an example, in zoo-based lowland gorilla maternal action, the following responses between mother and infant were seen (Hess, 1971): Daily minute genital inspection with rubbing, picking, and the like, by mother of male infant's genitals. Ears, face, shoulders, hands, feet, navel, were also minutely studied. The genitals were stroked, plucked at, moved to and fro. Sucking of genitals by ape mothers occurred, but was less frequent. The genital interest of the mother was paramount as after touching her infant's genital site she smelled her fingers.

In any cooperative studies between apes and humans, certain features of primate behavior have to be kept in mind as bearing on our own. Nadler (1939) has stated that "the higher the order of behavioral adaptiveness (broad intelligence), the more dominant the male of the species, the wider the range of copulatory responsiveness in the typical sexual cycle, and the greater the tendency of the female to respond accordingly to his advances irrespective of her sexual status." This is not politically correct!

This speaks to male dominance as the primary feature of primate development. From the viewpoint of the equality of the sexes, it provides a deterministic position that gives priority to male strength and aggression that is counter to our current enlightened social thinking.

As we discussed, it is our feeling that male aggression in humans, as a species, has been largely defused by female strategies that have utilized hidden estrus, pheromonal and visual stimuli to diffuse the aggression of male lust into limerant, long-term bonding. In zoos, females, when confined in close quarters with aggressive males, submit sexually without reference to desire. In a cage, there is no refuge from male aggression.

Unfortunately, many women are frequently treated like their "cousins" in the zoo. With or without the male's Viagara, depending on economics, jobs, and outside responsibilities, there is no escape from an aggressive human male within the confines of a restricted home environment, which can be similar to the shared cage in the zoo!

Sex in humans is frequently face-to-face, and as we encounter our lovers in the anterior position access to our pheromonal generators can be increased. On a face-to-face basis, while visual stimulation is most evident, pheromonal interactions must also be recognized.

Pygmy chimps (bonabos), like humans, practice ventral to ventral sex one third of the time. In the "missionary position," we humans can enjoy oral, olfactory, or tactile stimulation of the breasts. But pygmy chimps do not have breasts, which is not critical to their sexual behavior. With the exception of humans, breasts, for all other mammals, are primarily feeders, not strong sexual stimuli.

The breast deserves separate consideration as humans are the only mammal that has so eroticized the breast that we need to understand this obsession. Based on observation of our primate relatives, it is time that we provide other than Freudian explanations for the fixation-based or infantile hunger to explain our sexual interest in the mammary glands or their nipples.

We believe that sexual selection has led humans in large measure to the way we look. When naked, unlike the apes, with the exception of the chimpanzee, as males our sexual organs are largely visible. In women, the opposite is true, unless arousal is present. Unlike the female chimp, a woman's genitalia do not display unless stimulated. In chimpanzees, this stimulation begins during estrus with desire related to hormonal cycling, which with visible vaginal swelling provokes male response that is essentially a community affair.

We must be aware that in contrast, women keep both their estrus and stimulated sexual state as a concealed and largely private affair.

The behavior of the male rhesus monkey may be relevant to human behavior because what it signifies is that men may be less interested in a woman's overt sexual desire or needs, but what he responds to best are her sexual odors. While we are not monkeys it is highly probably that the odor stimulus of those women we hold close to us can stimulate our sexual overtures beyond a woman's readiness to copulate.

While we are not monkeys we are primates. Will our own future as human primates permit us to fully recognize our sexual and social needs? Aware of this, will we respect one another sufficiently to control our pheromonal signaling and the effects it has on our libido?

Chapter 4

"A kiss is a way of bringing into play Jacobson's organ and the limbic system as well as the more thoughtful cortex."
— **Lyall Watson,** *Jacobson's Organ*

"A kiss is a lovely trick designed by nature to stop speech when words become superfluous."
— **Ingrid Bergman**

The Intangible Attraction

Again, the greatest mystery that is a continuing recurrent theme in our lives is that which governs our sexuality. Our reproductive imperative is obvious but the impetus to couple is associated with a pleasure principle that transcends the physicality of us as creatures bonded skin to skin. What draws us to one another? While vision, voice, charm, physical prowess, and material goods play a decided role, for most of us there is an intangible influence that intoxicates us, that draws us together, beyond the rational lists that we create to justify our infatuation.

Could the irrational that converts friendship to passion relate to how we smell? Is our sexuality based on a genetically predetermined subconscious road map that equates hormonally stimulated body odors, pheromones, as a subtle influence produced by the one that attracts us? Is this the way we let that individual enter into the intimacy that leads to passion, bonding, and family?

Does our sexual image extend beyond our immediate frame to intrude on those capable of getting close to us? Why do we kiss? Why do we start with kissing and nuzzling and find ourselves entranced by our genital moisture as we, in our passion, work our way down the body that entrances us?

Is oral sex only a question of providing mutual reciprocal pleasure or is it trophic and essential to the passion necessary for love and even the perpetuation of our family values?

As a culture we find ourselves beset, on the one hand, by biblical values that have confined us to reproductive stereotypes, while on the other hand, with the availability of pornography, what was deemed to be perversion 50 years ago is now practiced by up to 50% of our adolescents. Is the increasing acceptance of oral sex an indication of the breakdown of family and religious values or can these patterns of sexual intimacies – often condemned in the past – be seen today as another way to strengthen the emotional bonds necessary for healthy relationships?

As a society concerned with the physiology of our behavior, as humans, cast in "God's image," must we always separate ourselves from our animal ancestry? How do we transcend our animal antecedents and reapply our instinctive drives necessary for reproduction and the development of our civilization? How do pheromones govern us, providing adaptation and contriving to produce constructive socialization?

In this chapter, we hold that pheromones (sexually responsive odor production) provides a repetitive stimulus to human love and attachment. It is obvious that we are no different at one level from our pets, or from farm animals, for whom genital odor is the root of reproductive interest. While this is not foreign to our behavior, it should not be destructive or demeaning to our values of love and concern for each other, but can be a reinforcing influence on family values. Pheromones stimulate sexual confidence and prepare the way for sexual excitement.

Essential to the development of human civilization, our preoccupation with pheromones has been held in check by the evolutionary development of the hidden estrus of our women. Unlike animal behavior, women sexually cycle without stimulating the obvious aggressive awareness of responding males. Our pheromonal odors, unlike those of insects, and all members of the animal kingdom, are subtle in their influence. We don't have to sniff odors to feel their influence, although we must draw close to be enveloped in them. Closeness is the key to our behavior governed by the trophic effects of pheromones on our brain. Yet, we cannot ignore the role they play, in governing the maturity of sexual identity, sexual pleasure, oral sex, and heterosexual or homosexual behavior. Our brains are pre-programmed to respond to this miasma that under the right circumstances envelops the human body and activates our subconscious for reproductive exploration. Sustained by pleasure, the subconscious envelops us and provides the need for physical fusion with the one that attracts us.

As a society we must be aware that human pheromones are being identified and made commercially available. Will our nose, our vomeronasal pheromonal detectors, now begin to occupy the place of our classical romantic heart? Is our nose, as it influences our brain, the true Valentine? Will gifts of pheromone scents replace chocolate candies in this new century?

We must learn to deal with pheromonal awareness, which will help to rationally explain disparate behavior previously dismissed as perversion. It is up to us to utilize our awareness of pheromones to see it as a new key to our subconscious that influence us beyond the Freudian cliches of Grecian mythology. Admittedly, problems are posed whenever we have to contend with instinctual drives that influence our unconscious. Will this new pheromonal awareness, which explains our sexual preferences, bonding and patterns of reproductive behavior, help us in the preservation of family values? Will pheromonal influences help explain rape and aggression; act to counter the loss of youthful attraction; and play a reinforcing role in affirmation of sexual identity and attractiveness?

Human pheromones are now available on the market, and so their role in our lives will be established during this century, and in this text we hope we will provide you with some insights into the "whys and wherefores" of pheromones as a new part of our identity.

Sex for every season

As Americans living in a postwar and postmodern era we are fully aware that sex is not just a matter of sexual reproduction. Indeed, everywhere one looks, whether it is in film, music videos, TV, or on the newsstand, we are constantly inundated with highly sexualized images and messages. If it were not enough to be immersed in a media blitz that emphasizes youth and sexuality, as humans, in addition we are simply designed for seeking to perpetuate sexual desire and pleasure. For instance, kissing is not just a reciprocal device incidental to or necessary for the final act of coitus, but a factor in the emotional ties that draws us together in long-lasting relationships. Those that don't use it as a social expression or as an act of bonding, in a sense deny the full expression of their human ancestry.

Our sexuality is beyond ape- or monkey-like behavior. We are not dependent on ovulation (estrus) to reproduce or pair for pleasure, and we are largely free of the promiscuous availability of partners, driven by a frenzy that acts to drive libido only when an egg is ready to be fertilized at the time of ovulation. Instead, we fixate strongly on one another's need for companionship as part of a pleasure-mediated event involving long-term social values that transcends sex as necessary only for reproduction!

In this age, our sexually expressive and liberated society, can observe that copulation often becomes subordinated to the broader process of oral lovemaking. Oral sex involves close nasal-genital contact directly related to genital olfactory stimulation. Lovemaking is not necessarily a seven-minute event, but is expanded by foreplay or post-coital activity where it can last beyond copulation with full appreciation of pheromonal production permeating our shared environment.

In this era where our sexuality is made visible beyond the bedroom or backseat of the automobile; now more increasingly visible by access to media exploitation and growing access to pornography, it becomes increasingly evident that sexual behavior is governed not only by procreation but also by pleasure.

Bruce Bagemihl summarizes the role of both homosexual and heterosexual behavior under the heading of "Biological Exuberance," (St. Martins Press, 1999) which speaks to the extraordinary energy of varied sexual behavior, both homosexual and heterosexual, throughout the animal kingdom. While at its center, exuberant sexual pursuits are motivated by the mechanics of reproduction and related to genetic factors governing species survival: In both human and mammalian terms, sexuality clearly is governed and defined by the pursuit of pleasure and pleasure can be equated with sexual odors that condition our shared environment.

Despite our concern for the spread of AIDS resulting in an ongoing holocaust in African nations, and its rapid spread to India, China, and Southeast Asia, our "biologic exuberance," can entrap us in lethal behavior that transcends religious or epidemiological stricture. Why is this so?

Time magazine recently presented data wherein 15% of our young adolescent girls and 45% of boys had experienced sexual intercourse. While 50% of both adolescent sexes have already experienced oral sex. Again, despite our rational human brain, we are like moths drawn to the flame of our sexual exuberance. While this is obviously related in some way to our species survival, it frequently places our personal survival or reputations in jeopardy. With pleasure at its core, why do 50% of us, including a former president, risking disgrace, indulge in oral sex despite his violation of ethics in a disturbing extra-marital affair?

Hedonism and Sexuality

One way we can classify our pheromonal responses is under the heading of "hedonism", the idea that pleasure, its absence, or the presence of pain determines the way we act. Pleasant or unpleasant experiences motivate us: For instance, dope addicts and nicotine addicts are motivated by a need for the pleasures of their drug of choice as well as the need to avoid the pain of its withdrawal. Both drug-using and normal behavior is further influenced by factors such as temperament, emotion and social affect which modulate our responses.

Human sexuality is also an addicting element in our lives, one that drives much of our behavior. We see the results of this in the human population expansion that threatens the precarious natural balance of our world. Yet despite the major governing role that sex plays in our individual lives and the world at large, our understanding and indeed our vocabulary of its expression in human beings remains limited. Bernard Arcard sums it up when he says:

"...Most societies recognize that sex is important, essential, powerful and sometimes even sacred—as if human beings, although very distant from one another, have all recognized that the sex act has an astonishing capacity to give pleasure, create life, and destroy it all at the same time. ...The sex act disarms us and places us in a position of vulnerability that requires discretion and even dissimulation. ...Our sexual behavior comes dangerously close to that of animals, and that it is therefore necessary to make it taboo in order to keep the essential distinction that separates us from them."

Oral sex

Again, our responses to pheromones are instinctual. For example, in the act of cunnilingus, as in fellatio, vision is no longer important to sexual behavior, and it is odor and the moist texture of our genitals that are limbic to our reaction. Our rational brain is overridden by our immersion in pheromones. Time stands still, daily problems vanish in the rush of pheromone odors released by moisture from odor-impregnated skin.

From an evolutionary standpoint, consider that kissing or nuzzling the breast of one's lover is probably not caused by a retrogressive oral fixation based on suckling, despite Freudian explanations to the contrary. It is most likely a broader manifestation of an evolved human need involving our preoccupation governing our contact with skin and its odor that was so important to our status as infants. In such behavioral responses, can modern psychiatry, devoid of Freudian allegations, aid us in the search for archetypal, pheromonal signals that can unite us and possibly also allay aggression?

If we become aware of pheromones how can we only equate kissing with a Freudian explanation that confines itself, in explanation, to a vestigial affinity for suckling at a mother's breast or bottle. Or, as "oral fixation," equating oral fixation with an atavistic desire for the joys of another spoonful of baby food or another go at the pacifier. If one looks at kissing and oral exchange in creatures as diverse as dogs and chimpanzees, one must find another explanation for the apparent pleasure of passionately kissing and exchanging saliva with the one that you love. The exchange of moisture is justified by its social role as an effort at bonding or reassurance and it is a broad based current event in the mammalian kingdom that transcends the human family.

Being sexy means being juicy

The essence of youthful sexuality is significantly governed by our ability to produce sexual secretions that are pheromone-laden. In summary, the final common denominator that governs sexuality requires that we be "juicy." When we are sexually aroused, we produce fluids, secretions or what the French call *mouille*. We literally become wet, juicy, or swollen in areas associated with sexual pleasure. This juiciness is designed to aid intromission. Aging is the converse: as we age, we dry up. Our skin and genitals lose their lubrication, pheromone production fails and skin loses its moisture and we lose our fervor.

In order to sustain our sexual health, we have to recapture both our ability to respond to and to reciprocate with sexually stimulated moisture. Sexual secretions transmit pheromonal odors that are both conscious and subconscious to our awareness. To paraphrase Alan Alda's character in *The Four Seasons*, "Sexuality is born in wetness," to which a character played by Rita Moreno responds, "It's easier that way." Indeed, it is not only our sexual "juice" that helps us in the actual physical mechanics of sexual intercourse, but the ability to produce these secretions serves as both an impetus and a way to sustain healthy sexual desire. Moisture abets sexual performance, and provides olfactory pleasure, which serves to reinforce emotional interest in our partner.

Seen from a different light, consider that for many people, odor awareness often declines with advancing age. In some cases this loss of odor awareness has been blamed on zinc deficiency that also relates to loss of taste and the problems of immuno-deficiency. Loss of smell awareness is a diagnostic loss that is a defining factor in Alzheimer's and Parkinson's disease. Whatever the inter-related physiologic mechanisms that govern the maintenance of our youth or sexuality, we need to be able to smell and be smelled. One of the first symptoms of Alzheimer's disease, senile dementia, is the loss of odor awareness before intellectual loss may be clearly apparent.

Sexual selection

We must be aware that our evolutionary heritage may have been governed by eons of sexual choice. Geoffrey Miller proposes in *The Mating Mind* (Doubleday, New York, 2000) that humans achieved their large brains as the result of sexual selection. He suggests that two million years ago we went from a one-pound (Chimpanzee-sized) brain to our current three-pound brain because women in places like Oldavi Gorge in Africa preferred to mate with smart men. It was not unlike the peahen selecting the peacock with the most ornate tail, only in this case, both sexes benefited from the female's choice in mating selection based on a male's performance governed by intelligence (charm and wit) or his resultant food gathering success, as the brain dominating choice. We believe that pheromonal selection was also an evolutionary adaptation.

We agree with Geoffrey Miller that women helped steer evolution by showing a preference for intelligent men but, moreover, we believe sexual selection was also directed by pheromonal attraction. All other factors being equal (imaginative cave paintings, exceptional hunting skills, eloquence, wearing animal furs, or jewelry, lighting fires), both sexes have also been led by their noses, to their sexual partners and together, they have selected the ones that they most enjoyed being with (and smelling.) But, we cannot ignore other factors entirely, either:

If a woman's choice of mate was governed by her perception of a male's intelligence, does this have any relevance to our current problems with intellectual jealousy that may be at the root of ethnic, national, or individual antagonism? Intelligence can be perceived as wealth, and it can possibly be just as important as a contribution to competitive jealousy related to athletic performance or beauty. Do some of us resent our seemingly more brilliant neighbors because of a subconscious awareness that demonstrates that cerebral brilliance can be subconsciously seen as a manifestation intellectually establishing an element of sexual competition. Paradoxically, are some of our high school honor students rejected by peers for the competitive fear that they might also become sexual rivals? ("The Weakest Link" presents this in a television quiz show competition.)

Size does matter

It is not only pheromones that contribute to sexual selection: there is also the compelling attraction of physical appearance. Although only a current factor in "outhouse humor," one of these compelling factors may be penis size. Among primates, men have the largest penis. A male gorilla with an erection successfully utilizes a one-and a half-inch penis with the help of his female consorts. The chimpanzees do well with three and a half inches, while men sport five to six inches of erectile tissue. To explain this, penile size is dictated by the timely production of the male hormone dihydrotestosterone. This is metabolically derived from the libido-stimulating male hormone, testosterone, which is also largely provided by our brains derived from the neurocrine hormonal production of pregnenalone and dehydroepiandrosterone (DHEA). Both pregnenalone and DHEA are produced in greatest quantities by the human brain. And both of these hormones, which lead to the production of our sex hormones, testosterone and estrogen, enhance neurite formation which stimulate nerve interconnections. DHEA, also increases nitric oxide (NO) formation that increases blood flow in the brain. These hormones when given to rodents, enhance their maze running ability. In addition, pregnenalone,

DHEA, testosterone, and estrogen serve to make us feel good. They act as natural antidepressants, and are produced by both sexes, with production declining with age.

DHEA and its precursor, pregnenalone, decline with age, stress, and chronic illness.   DHEA has significant anti-stress activity and all these neurocrine hormones improve memory performance while acting to maintain our genital sensitivity and our juiciness, i.e. the moisture and turgor of our skin. DHEA, like Viagra, can release nitric oxide, which causes vasodilation and increased blood flow.

Did pre-historic women select mates for their intelligence, or embarrassing to consider, were our early ancestors influenced by the size of a prospective mate's penis? It doesn't matter, as both elements of selection probably led to our dominant brains. Genital size reflects on pheromonal output. The more sexually responsive skin or mucous membrane we have, the more glandular sebaceous secretions available to govern sexual selection and the production of pheromones or copulins that influenced the bonding between the sexes.

This raises another question: the broad access of our prominent nose, in place of a muzzle may have developed not only because of human evolution which led to an upright posture, but may have also developed as a response to finding the most appropriate mate. Our noses act as receptors that can focus to interact closely to genital and body odors as an adjunct to visual stimulation. Remember, women have a hidden estrus: we don't flaunt our ovulatory access with dramatic color changes or swelling of the vagina, genital area, or buttocks, as is the case in other primates (i.e. chimps and baboons).

As women achieved an upright posture with large supporting buttock muscles, necessary for walking, their genitals became "hidden," unless deliberately exposed in the supine ("missionary") position. Did men need a more prominent nose as an olfactory detecting apparatus, a "range finder," to recognize the sexual availability of the opposite sex? Did this follow from our having achieved an upright posture that distances us from our neighbor's private, hidden genitalia? Did humans, in contrast to dogs, stop sniffing each other's genitals because our noses did not have to be that close to the groin area, as is true in the case of our pets, for us to be aware of sexual attraction or availability? Did our interest in pheromones lead to our distinctive proboscis? Did we develop sinus cavities not only to warm the air we breathe but also to extract its scent? Did males retain facial hair as a wick to emit and absorb sexual odors? To entertain the female scent? Does this explain the strategic grooming of body, underarm, and pubic hair?

Can we accept pheromonal production and sensitivity as a major stimulus to our long-term bonding with the opposite sex that establishes our familial interest necessary for sustaining our children? Do our large brains, distinct noses, intelligence, familial and social structures depend on our evolutionary response to sexually-derived odors? We believe the answer to all of these questions is a resounding "Yes!"

Freud, sexual perversion, and the "erect nose"
What if Freud had focused on body odor as the primary factor in explaining sexual preferences in adult life rather than the oral or anal stages of early childhood development? The entire history of psychoanalysis and our understanding of human behavior would be fundamentally different.

It is fascinating to think that it could have gone this way. Wilhelm Fliess was a colleague and friend of Freud, who had a profound influence on Freud and is credited with conveying to Freud his concepts of juvenile sexuality, bisexuality, and repression. Fliess felt that there were areas of nasal tissue with "erectile" properties similar in nature to our genitals. He claimed that our nasal mucosa behaved similarly to the hormone-sensitive tissue in the uterus, which respond to the menstrual cycle.

Despite Freud's awareness of infantile sexuality and his enthusiastic support of Wilhelm Fliess' (1897) concept of the nose as a sexually sensitive (hormone responsive) organ, Freud denigrated the sexual role of odor in human behavior. He classified as "prurient" any sexual interest in odor, which along with masturbation, was considered a "perversion,"—attitudes which, thanks to his influence, still color much of our thinking.

In an 1897 letter to Fliess (Masson, Freud, 1985), Freud firmly shut the door on odor as governing sexual identity, behavior, or passionate attachment within a normal context. He stated that "the abandonment of former sexual zones was linked to the changed part played by sensation of smell: upright walking, nose raised from the ground, at the same time a number of formerly interesting sensations attached to the earth becoming repulsive—(i.e. odor). The zones which no longer produce a release of sexuality in normal and mature human beings are the anus and the mouth and throat. This is to be understood in two ways; first, that seeing and imagining these zones no longer produce an exciting effect, and second, that the internal sensations arising from them make no contribution to the libido, the way the sexual organs proper do. In animals, these sexual zones continue in force in both respects; if this persists in human beings too, perversion results."

If Freud is right, we are all "perverted". Stoddard, in his book, The Scented Ape points out that the axillae (the arm pits) are strong generators of sexual odors from glands situated in this area. Again, we also produce odors from glands in our face, scalp, chest and, of course, our genitalia.

If Freud had given attention to the importance of olfaction, it is likely that we would have long since developed more physiologically grounded concepts of sexual behavior. Psychiatric therapeutic intervention would have involved an interest in pheromones. The sexual basis of neurosis might then have included a chemosensory focus, (i.e., olfaction), and human behavioral studies would have included major chapters focusing on the role of smell in the practice of psychoanalysis.

Female orgasm

Throughout evolution, women have selected male partners based on many factors: intelligence, strength, attractiveness, and, yes, penis size. By doing so, women directly influenced sexual selection. As Geoffrey Miller makes clear, penis size does matter, but, what he and others, including Freud have missed, however, is the important role that oral sex plays in contributing to the establishment of emotional ties that can lead to the long-term bonding needed for reproductive success.

Oral sex, in particular, allows the clitoris to take center stage, as the act of cunnilingus provides women an opportunity to experience orgasms that are often not possible through vaginal penetration alone. While it is taken for granted that for most men, sexual intercourse often results in male orgasm, this is not always the case for women. The penis isn't always necessary to satisfy our female partners, while it is central to a man's sexual gratification. Men from prehistoric times have been drawn towards women based on their physical attractiveness, ability to bear children, and for the sexual pleasures that accompany an intimate relationship. During oral sex, the clitoris again is a central attraction in its ability to produce pheromones that are hard to ignore. In this regard, vaginal penetration is only one way to achieve satisfaction for one's partner. While vaginal orgasm may be attainable, a man's ability to pleasure his woman lover is often dependent on him finding the clitoris and G-spot that results in vaginal lubrication, sexual intercourse via penetration and/or a clitoral orgasm.

We believe that female orgasm is important not only in an evolutionary sense, in its contribution to help establish long-term bonding, but in the sense that it has contributed to the nature of satisfying oral sex for both parties. Men engage in oral sex with their women partners in part, because they are attracted by the erotic vagina, made that way by the sexual odors it produces. This attraction often leads to oral sex and orgasm for the woman and can contribute to the intimacy and bonding between couples that is necessary for a long-term paired relationships.

Aside from the sexual gratification, orgasm provides a vehicle for increased opportunity for fertilization and reproductive success. Orgasm plays a role in sperm retention by decreasing "backflow" preventing the loss of sperm by inducing vaginal spasms that may be critical to a successful pregnancy. The main contribution of the penis relates to sperm distribution and although it contributes to sexual pleasure, this pleasure must be shared with your partner in order for it to help establish emotional intimacy considering the period of child bearing and nursing that inconveniences sexual pleasure. By strengthening a couple's sexual pleasure, oral sex may provide an alternative that might also limit a man's interest in polygamy.

Allaying aggression

Sex has been compared to a rose bush; you have to get past the thorns to reach the roses. The thorns represent the problem of male aggression and territoriality. Again, this explains the development of elaborate mating displays in animals to displace aggression or in humans via dances or by changes in body display. Another common mechanism for turning aggression to courtship is for either partner to assume childlike behavior that results in the solicitation of feeding. This is seen very often in birds as well as in chimpanzees and dogs. Taking it one step further, we feel that human behavior follows a similar pattern: With courtship we exchange gifts, such as candy and flowers on Valentine's Day. When one is in search of a sexual relationship, we seek to elicit from each other various childlike patterns of behavior. Many of us, in the early glow of infatuation find ourselves calling our beloved unusual "pet names," and even speaking to them in high-pitched singsong tones, much the way we would speak to small animals or small children. We dance together or seek admiration and desire in athletic, dress or intellectual display, just like courting birds.

The silent language of the body or our facial expression defines our awareness of others and conveys our attitude. In African monkeys facial coloring and the coloring or swelling of the rump are a communicating system between the sexes. In humans we feel that pheromones can play that role.

In birds, dogs, cats and tigers, response to strangers of their own species is met with male aggression, particularly during the mating period. This overt hostility must be defused, to avoid competitive male aggression that can spill over to hurt not only combative males, but available females, despite the need for mating to occur. When an estrus female appears on the scene, despite her sexual availability, male instinct may initially perceive her as a stranger, unless behavioral patterns are instinctively established which convert male aggression to courtship. Aggressive males have to rapidly switch from hostility to courtship, and the signals emitted by available females govern this response. Similarly, males must signal their peaceful intentions to females through courtship behavior, to participate in displays that signal their sexual availability, which will not be preempted by the primacy of aggression.

Can a woman's pheromones dispel male aggression? With rape it might serve as the wrong signal. Yet, how many of us in the presence of the one we love achieve a tranquility that has at its core the awareness of sexual excitement. True, there are exceptions where masochism and sadistic behavior are associated with human sexuality, but one must ask if familial bonding and civilization resulted from pheromonal attraction damping down aggression by providing for the anticipation or prolongation of pleasure as a mutually shared human event.

As we have seen earlier, the ability of pheromones to encourage love between mother and child is also seen in the intimate bonding between lovers. How could it not be, as we spend much of our time in each other's pheromonal-laden company? It's not surprising that in sharing ideas, activities, and eventually our beds, that we would become emotionally connected on a physiological level through the exposure and exchange of our pheromones. Pheromones are "biphasic" in their effects. At one level they may stimulate aggression, but more commonly at another place and time they may transmit an aura of peaceful affability, leading to the "Garden of Eden" and the passion of coitus and its afterglow.

Alpha Males and Females

The Alpha male or dominant male, as defined by sociologists, is the male animal that within the framework of intragroup competition over access to limited resources comes out on top. He is the "top dog", the one that dominates the pack or group because of his social skills or aggressive strength. The Alpha male's dominance results in greater access to food and females for reproduction. Alpha females possess the same advantages as alpha male, with the added advantage that they provide a better environment or social structure for their progeny.

It is our observation that Bill Clinton represents what we so readily see in alpha males: leadership and dominance, which enhances access to females even under the most restricted circumstances. We recognize this behavior when we look at animal species as diverse as pigeons, fish, lizards, lions, sheep, elephants, monkeys and the great apes. The dominant male has a higher level of the male hormone (testosterone) and aggressively defends his turf motivated by food or sexual desire. In our society where we are supposed to control our sexual aggression, the territorial aspect of alpha male behavior must be controlled to avoid exploitation of the innocent, jealousy, and questions of paternity.

Alpha males communicate their dominance through display - - a large rack on a buck, Schwarzenegger's muscles, the chin dimple of both Kirk and Michael Douglas – and odor. The scent of a dominant male attracts the females of the species and discourages would-be competitive males. Women who are odor-aware invariably describe the scent of a "strong" man as "sweet".

Alpha dogs have their counterparts in the queen bee. The female bee that ends up dominating the hive develops faster in the egg and hatches first. She puts out pheromones that shut down the development of other females and kills those that are crawling up her tail even as she is emerging from the egg. She can tell her female competitors by their smell.

Pseudomales

Creatures as diverse as cockroaches, fish, birds, sheep, monkeys, and stags engage in male competition for female sexual attention. In this regard alpha males possess the pheromones and visual appeal that attract the attention of the opposite sex. Not all males are alpha and there are unfortunate males that do not have what it takes to compete successfully for female attention or to prevail over rivals. In mammals, like us, this relates to the male hormone testosterone. The levels of this hormone are increased by success in combat and diminished with failure.

In our human society men and women can boost their level of testosterone through victory or successful intimidation. If intimidated or a loser you decrease your testosterone production. Unfortunately, many of us are victims of Pseudomales who maintain their testosterone levels by pushing other people around. True males know and are confident in their maleness. You can always tell a "Pseudomale" by his efforts at intimidation and control. Pseudomales frequently wind up as bureaucratic chiefs, wife beaters, or dictatorial heads of state who maintain their self image through persecution or aggression of those weaker than themselves.

In the future we may be able to determine Pseudomale candidates with a pheromone odor detector. Alternatively we can neutralize their aggression by adorning ourselves with the right dominant scent that can either provide us with a victorious image or lead to intimidation of our rivals.

Bonding between lovers

We maintain that we as humans are not desensitized to sexual odors, but that we must get closer to the source of sexual odors for them to be effective. Unlike dogs and other animals, who respond to odors at great distances, or via signal posts based on urinary or fecal deposits, we humans have to be close to the pheromone's living source to respond.

Put another way, in order for us to be "turned on," we must be able to detect and exchange pheromones with our beloved. We believe that the mechanism of pheromonal communication is so compelling and prevalent that we believe that it is largely responsible for the reason why two people are successfully drawn together and remain together.

This is not hard to understand: your loyalty to your mate is served by sexual stimulation and this satisfaction has to be seen as based fundamentally on sexual attraction and behavior that expresses this attraction, including oral sex, beginning with kissing. Kissing as a romantic or bonding event, as distinct from its social or ceremonial role (bussing or hand kissing), can only occur if odor affinities are in effect. It is our observation that sexual morality apart from its religious, family, and legal base is governed by pheromones, which can stabilize relationships or, in contrast, can create episodes of passionate digression, rape, and immorality.

Again, we believe that oral sex is not a perversion! We are not odor-desensitized but *odor particularized*. We are highly sensitive to odors, including sexual odors. We respond to the pheromonal scent that occupies our cerebral "love map." Although the reproductive imperative drives us together, for humans it is not copulation alone that is the end in itself. Despite social or religious condemnation, oral sex and it's emotional ties contributes to our need to propagate which requires that we bond together and create a family unit. For passion or love to express itself in a way that can hold us to each other, we must get close to our partners to be enveloped in their "odor environment" that makes us feel at home.

When we are physically close to one another, it is our sexual odors that draw us together! While there may or may not be a conscious awareness of this pheromonal interplay occurring, what normally follows in response to our pheromonal envelope is touching and this, in turn, often stimulates further sexual arousal that further enhances the pheromonal environment which gives rise to the subconscious expression of our sexual behavior.

As pair-bonded mates, we become intoxicated with each other, and then addicted to each other. While there are moments in our lives where as adolescents we can love from afar and knighthood and religion had their codes of chivalry and honor that intentionally left sex to the imagination. For love to truly take hold, we need to be aware of and be able to exchange our sexual odors. That's what romance is all about! Romance is triggered by odor to produce the yin/yang of a relationship. This is based on excitement, "biological exuberance," with its accompanying paradox: excitement in a sexual relationship makes you want to draw near and stay in the presence of the one you love. However, once in the presence of your loved one you are excited within but, if love is realizable, tranquil without. It can be the sexual odor of our partner that does this for us. We are developmentally prepared for this by our odor-mediated neonatal experience at the breast of our mother and in the bosom of our family where the smells that immerse us condition and nurture our long-term relationships. While our skin and genitals may crave erotic attention conditioned by visual and pheromonal stimulation, our drawing together is also tranquilized by the narcotic influence, the endorphin, opiate-like effects released by the object of our desire that holds us to them.

Again, oral sex is significant to human bonding and should not be seen as a perversion, as it provides essential evidence of how we are uniquely sexually expressive beyond what one sees in almost any other animal. While reproduction and species survival is the evolutionary goal and our sexuality requires commitment and family structure for us to maintain our species. Again, we as humans are *odor particularized*, meaning we are influenced by sexual odors that stimulate and direct our reproductive success and long term commitments.

Although the reproductive imperative brings us together, it is not sexual intercourse alone, despite the reproductive focus of its religious value that is the end in itself. This need for us to propagate requires that we join together to create a family unit. This provides the religious justification for our sexual interest in each other. We must not ignore that pheromonal influences make this possible and these effects are most manifest in our spontaneous behavior that makes kissing, hugging, and oral genital contacts pleasurable. Sexual intercourse, depending on intromission for its Judeo-Christian religious value is biologically only one part of our human concerns.

One must also consider that the genital focus that produces and creates sexual odor, the matrix of our bonding, has led to the prominence of orgasm as a feature of our sexual existence because the clitoris and penis are at the center of genital odor attraction. It is both mouth to mouth, as in kissing, and oral-genital contact that may, even more than the act of copulation itself, lead to prolongation of sexual excitement and eventually orgasm.

Although there is growing social awareness of this, it's importance to our understanding of our evolutionary development and how this affects our human behavior has only recently been grasped. No other animal is as involved in oral sex as humans. To understand this unique aspect of our behavior requires that we recognize this facet of our being as a factor in human evolution. Oral sex, which begins with kissing and works its way down, should not be seen as an anathema to religious doctrine, but as an adjunct to what is necessary that can add to love and familial affinities. We must also be aware that steroid secretions from genital, axillary and other sites may convey moods that govern mutual interaction and communication.

Although it's not readily apparent there are chemical homologies between odors. Odors are made of distinct volatile chemical structures that impinge on receptors in our nose that influence brain centers to produce stereotypical patterns of behavior. Bad odors repel us while those that are attractive draw us to them. Adaptively, odors tell us when food is bad, or attract us to their source as indicative of good food or sex. Odors are volatile, they float in the wind, rise from food, dung, or the sweat and secretions from our bodies. A slight change in an odor molecular structure or in its concentration, as seen in moths, can alter perception and our attitudes towards our environment. Thus, undergarments, smelly feet, or unwashed genitals, depending on the intensity of their odor, attracts some people and repels most of us. In addition, attitudes or conditioning experiences can convert an unpleasant odor to a pleasant one and vice-versa.

Evolution does not necessarily mean that we abandon the past, but rather that we modify its physiological expression. The human response to pheromones is instinctive. It functions in similar fashion to what we see in newborn babies who mimic the facial expressions of their mothers as an instinctive response. They also smile instinctively in the same manner. This inborn behavior governs mutual exchange of emotions whose impact with reinforcement contributes to childhood and adult patterns of social exchange and conditioning.

In *The Scented Ape,* Stoddard (1990) presents a comparative picture between the behavior of the great apes and humans. Among our genetically similar relatives, like the ordinary chimpanzee, there is an aggressive shared sexuality between females and males with little male participation in pair bonding. This is unlike what is seen in the pygmy chimp, the bonobo subspecies that resembles us in many ways. In contrast to the human condition, in the great apes behavior that govern sexuality are primarily visual, vocal, or seen in grooming. In our closest genetic relative, the chimp, as in the baboons, with ovulation or estrus, the female genital skin swells and becomes distinctly visible as a red marker. Visual and vocal signaling brings the sexes together for sexual activity, but primatologists give little emphasis to odor clues as long-term bonding factors in the great apes.

Similarly, when it comes to humans, we are closest to the apes, and Stoddard feels, along with Geoffrey Miller, that we as a human society progressed based on the female predominant choice of her male partner. As we humans evolved from our ape-like progenitors, there was a decrease in the sole importance of visible signals as in an ovulatory- or estrus-focused sexuality based on swollen or colored genitalia. Atavistically, this attractiveness is still visible in the appeal of pornography or "girlie magazines," where vulval, "pink" became a hot selling factor to stimulate males to purchase Hustler beginning in the 60s, but obviously, this is not a socially visible factor before intimacy, bonding and sexual activity are present. Genital attraction is still an embarrassment to most of us.

Again, human sexual development led to a de-emphasis on overt visible aggressive sexuality, which defused male competition for females. With the estrus no longer on public display, the female's fertile period was transformed into a private event, hidden within her body. This probably led to our more stable family structure that provided an environment suitable for child rearing, resulting in furthering our complex social development and our civilization. The above was accomplished, despite menstruation, by the decline in gross cyclic changes in a woman's visible sexual skin. Stoddard felt that, in contrast to our position in this text, that there had to be an accompanying decline in sexual odor awareness associated with the concealment of estrus. We disagree!

We must emphasize that it is our feeling that odor is still an important sexual attractant, despite concealment, but we have to get closer to one another to be aware of its impact.

Instead of periodic female availability, human males were rewarded by the relatively constant sexual availability of women independent of their state of fertility. In humans, female sexuality was no longer dependent on their hormonal signals that an egg was ready to be fertilized. If male to female relationships became a long-term consort or bonding event, copulation became a frequent event statistically assuring that an egg would eventually become available to be fertilized.

The development of the private estrus has enabled non-dominant human males to mix with approachable females without the fear of physical competitive aggression from other males. Similarly, women did not have to, on occasion, hide from aggressively sexual males. If not for this, the nature of our sexual relationships would be very different: male sexual harassment or female-instituted sexual aggression would be the norm during the estrus phase of a woman's hormonal cycle, as is seen in chimpanzees. However, even in chimpanzees sexual intercourse can, on occasion, occur outside the specific period of ovulation when sexual exchange is at its most appealing.

Estrus

In contrast to human estrus, which is hidden, in Old World monkeys, chimps and to a lesser extent gorillas, orangutans and gibbons, related sexual swelling and prominence of their genitalia occurs with ovulation. In the apes, estrus is most marked in the chimpanzee, in which the labia actually swell sufficiently to add significant depth to the true vagina. Estrus, absent in humans, blatantly announces its presence in female monkeys and the great apes. The advantages of announcing to males that a female is sexually accessible are as follows:

1. There is an increase in female opportunities to mate with many males.
2. The stimulation of sexual competition provides mating opportunities with the strongest or most effective males.
3. This permits ovulation to be noted, so that the paternal investment in the female is clearly related to her

pregnancy and its resultant offspring, in a manner that the father or primary or alpha male can identify with, so that he is aware that the progeny are his, making male parenting possible.

4. Swelling of genitals provides a site for pheromonal release. In effect, vascular engorgement of the female perineum may be likened to an incense burner in its capacity to release pheromonal odors.

In contrast, in women, labial swelling or tumescence of both labia majora and minora is associated only with their reaching sexual maturity and responding to sexual excitement. While cyclic genital and vaginal swelling is not important for a human seasonal or monthly cyclic sexual attraction, the swelling and moistening of this tissue based on desire, prepares the way to coitus by providing lubrication and pleasant friction, but it also, we contend, contributes odor to set the emotional stage for both short- and long-term relationships that can mollify aggression and produce bonding in sexually predatory males.

Although male gibbons, the lesser apes, are monogamous, and although estrus governs gibbon female sexual responsiveness, copulation can occur outside of the ovulatory peak; in other words, monogamy is not completely precluded by the cyclicity of estrus.

Humans have lost estrus as a visible event, and it is of interest that across human society, this may have led to developments that have determined that the bulk of the world's cultures are polygynous in that they allow men to have more than one wife at a time. Polygamy, obviously increases the odds for finding an ovulating mate. However, in our Western society we practice serial polygamy with the sanction of divorce. Despite the development of Judeo-Christian values, humans are demonstrably and predominately polygamous, and this is true despite our hidden estrus, cyclic menstruation, and the advantage provided by the sexual availability of women outside the ovulatory cycle.

We must ask, apart from the attractive interaction of pheromones, if polygamy or the serial polygamy of divorce will remain as primarily a male-dominated choice based on physical, financial, and institutional control? Will we see, with greater equality of the sexes, the demonstration that infidelity and promiscuity are social problems of equal sexual responsibility in both sexes? If sexuality is governed by pheromonal attraction, will the future find the means to unleash, in a controlled fashion, pheromones to enhance the impact of odor on our social structures of marriage and family?

In contrast to the broad sexual availability of women, we know that estrus makes non-human female mammals available sexually only periodically. For example, for dogs and cats this is several times a year. In cows, availability is on a short monthly cycle. In elephants, it can occur in four-year cycles. Sexual availability ends with estrus and coitus, but pregnancy and lactation result in events that limit female availability and force males to seek out other approachable females. Lactation suppresses ovulation and female estrus. "Female chimps in heat mate as often as six times a day with as many as seven males in succession for a total of several hundred times for each baby conceived," writes Bagemihl.

Again, by keeping her estrus quiet, a primitive human female could select her mate without having to fend off numerous frenetic suitors. With her hidden estrus, she could exercise selection of males based not only on the stimulus of a male's physical releasers, but on the size of their brains as well. As Stoddard first suggested, hidden estrus offered the human species an opportunity to avoid the problems of fratricide by giving primitive women a chance to select their mates on a one-to-one basis. Thus, women were given the opportunity to respond to intelligence or looks as factors in mate selection apart from dependence on the sheer physical brawn and aggression of the dominant male. (Although male dominance as discussed earlier may have also related to neuro-endocrine sexual hormonal impact on brain development.)

A woman's freedom to choose

It cannot be emphasized too strongly that a hidden estrus may have allowed women to help steer evolution by freeing them to engage in sexual intercourse throughout their menstrual cycles. It is not an exaggeration to say that this is evolutionarily important as it greatly influenced our sexual development through history. Moreover, the hidden estrus may have enabled women to select male sexual partners according to their own criteria. We agree with Miller that women selected men based on their intelligence, as well as their brawn and obvious display of physical sexual attractiveness.

The key to the importance that a hidden estrus in women plays is as follows: it allows the woman to be selective and in the long run, as discussed, her choices have helped steer evolution. In the absence of an overwhelming focused sexual desire related to estrus, couples can slip away at will, avoiding the frenetic copulating crowd. (This consort activity is seen in the bonobo, or pygmy chimp.) This has allowed for female selectivity in mating that permitted choice to be made of brainy as distinct from brawny males. Without the frenzy of estrus to complicate matters, aggression can be minimized as a determinant in the selection of a mate.

Sexual competition

To recapitulate, in lieu of strong sexual odors and pink vaginal displays, a concealed, discrete estrus is easier on males. It is obvious that sexual competition in most animals can be hazardous or even life threatening to male survival. In most species, males fight bloodily to achieve dominance in an effort to gather estrus females for themselves. A dramatic example of this is seen in mountain sheep. The males, willing to fight for "first dibs" on the available ewes may act to the point of shortening their life spans.

Male mountain sheep have only a life expectancy of nine and a half years. They fight desperately for females in heat, which often results in serious physical injury. To lose in this battle for dominance damages males endocrinologically and emotionally. If they lose in the competition, they decrease their output of testosterone, the male hormone that contributes to their feelings of sexual well-being and fighting capacity. There is, however, the fate of a smaller group of males who suffer from chronic lungworm infection. These sick males do not have the respiratory reserve to fight for females. They wait for the dominant male to win his battle and then mount the female after the stud male leaves. These weaker males take their turn at mating with a 50% chance of impregnating the female despite her previous copulation with a dominant male. These non-competitive males can live on the average of 10 more years than the aggressive, healthy, fighting stud rams. Do studs die prematurely and do these "sick," less dominant males perpetuate mountain sheep intelligence by cleverly avoiding physical battle?

By extension, we can understand how a low-key estrus but with focal pheromonal odors of limited radius, served to protect human males from killing each other to obtain approachable mates. To attract males, human females have to cultivate a physical closeness for reproduction to occur and this requires an evolutionary decline in male aggression as a key factor necessitating their coital need to find and impregnate females. Female selection and bonding of males to females became a part of our pheromonal heritage when close proximity to sexual mediating odor became necessary. Although, as humans we have not completely removed sexual aggression from our behavioral pattern we have dampened it down, but its persistence may be evidence of our aggressive animal ancestry.

In evolution, sexual selection plays an important part in molding the appearance of males and females. While humans are not selected for antlers, observing adolescent behavior, where girls are attracted to the muscular athletes, or boys to the pretty cheerleaders, this demonstrates that physical elements are clearly involved in the selection process. Large breasts, areola, narrow waists, and big hips and buttocks became an alluring stimulus for human males that provided a launching pad to accommodate the odor pheromonal assault on the male libido.

Courtship Rituals

In gorillas, the estrus female staring at the silverback male of her desire elicits a response from the male. Staring is part of female gorillas courtship behavior during estrus. Humans behave similarly, when attracted. We gaze in sustained fashion at one another, our pupils dilate and our susceptibility to the opposite sex is based strongly on vision. To that we must add a pheromonal element, which brings our noses and our bodies in orientation to the fragrance of skin and genitalia. This should not be surprising if one perceives kissing as a pheromone-mediated event. How many of us, thrilled with kissing, find ourselves sexually aroused and our genitals responding and yet we don't know why this is happening? How many lovers luxuriate in the sexual odors of their loved ones which on touching or embracing and fondling the genitals, find that these odors cling to hands, hair, and clothing?

By reducing the physical distance between individuals, pheromones and the excitement they arouse reaches us. By decreasing the importance of the broad sexual arousal of estrus that leads to male aggression involving the entire community, evolution has permitted humans to enjoy each other sexually largely devoid of physical violence.

Thanks to evolution and its modulation by sexual selection with a hidden estrus, and a limited range to pheromonal dissemination, male reproductive success did not have to reside in wrestling females physically away from competitors, or in intimidating the competition, but could also relate to providing subtle sensory clues, that encompass what we now identify with intellect and charm. Does intellect affect pheromonal output? Can intelligence stimulate genital secretions in equal fashion to the sexual arousal that is stimulated by the display of sexy muscles, athletic performance, the timbre of voice or an alluring cleavage or shapely hips? If so, here was the true beginning of civilization!

In humans, the almost constant sexual availability of women, when unencumbered by childbearing, whether we are monogamous or polygamous, requires that males provide sufficient sperm to rise to the occasion. This has given humans in evolutionary primate selection, a scrotum second only to the chimpanzee in size. With closeness provided by male-female bonding, sperm volume, or sperm competition is not dependent on the number of competitive males competing for sperm access to the same vagina with its waiting egg.

As previously discussed, in Darwinian terms, during early sexual evolution, a large penis may have been attractive to women, even as a large bust or shapely buttocks is a turn-on for men, yet is there more to the equation here than meets the eye? Women have large breasts and/or prominent areolae surrounding the nipple, which are virtually nonexistent in apes and monkeys. Why? Again, it's about pheromone production. Why are we richly endowed with prominent breasts and aerola as well as impressive penis length and large testicles? We must be reminded that our penises, testes, vaginas and, indeed, the entire perineum, as well as breasts, areolae, and axillae are seeded with odor-producing glands. Aside from the obvious visual appeal that these physical attributes provide, they also are capable of producing the sexual secretions, the human miasma that is needed for sexual arousal and emotional bonding to occur between two people. This may also be true for the retention of scalp, facial, or body hair, which is no longer needed for warmth but provides for adornment and acts as a wick to retain or deliver pheromones.

Again, this explains why sex in humans is so frequently face-to-face. When we face our lovers, the central position of our pheromonal skin generators enhances breast and genital odor availability and production. On a face-to-face basis, while visual stimulation is most evident, pheromonal interactions must also be recognized. The scalp, face, neck, and underarms are also pheromone generators.

We believe that sexual selection has led humans in large measure to evolve the way we look. Again, unlike the female chimp, a woman's genitalia are not readily displayed unless she is stimulated, but once nude and sexually responsive, the pubic region is quite apparent for both aesthetic visual and odor input.

Consider, if you will, the analogies in our own behavior as parallel to the attraction of the male marmoset, a monkey-related creature, for the urine of their estrus or pregnant female. Going back in evolutionary time, a primitive male, designed to exercise reproductive imperatives on any approachable female if he found one that looked good and smelled good, might find sexual odors as an inducement to hang around. Pheromones now become stimuli to nesting. This is particularly true in early humans if the female was sexually available at all times and not dependent on estrus to stimulate us both sexually and frenetically for a short sexual holiday each month or especially during springtime. With pheromones as an aesthetic influence, if in addition, our prospective mate provided grooming behavior or touch that was focused on genital stimulation, long term interest would be further enhanced.

Monogamy, however, is not necessarily a determinant of human behavior. Although male gibbons and simians, lesser apes, are monogamous, estrus still governs their dependence on female sexual responsiveness. Based on this, monogamy is not precluded or influenced by response to estrus. In contrast to the gibbon, as seen in human societies, we are mainly polygamous. In our Western society, we practice serial monogamy, a form of polygamy, with sanction of divorce. To decrease the incidence of divorce or to enhance our sexual lives we must search for an understanding of the bonds that can keep us together. Our commandments proscribing adultery which laud maternal or filial piety can be strengthened by pheromonal understanding, which can be physically applied to maintain long-term attraction between couples.

In summary, unlike estrus-dependent animals, women are generally sexually available or accede to male importuning despite pregnancy, lactation, or even "a sick headache." In our case, men, with all our sexual frustrations and petulant desire, have to be thankful that we don't have to place ourselves in grave danger in competitive pursuit of blatantly estrus women.

 Tied by pregnancy to dependence on men in a hunter-gatherer early society a woman's selection of a mate, and her ability to sustain his interest, had to have a long-term sexual base beyond romance. Sexuality, related to short-term coitus that led to long-term involvement, was necessary to make the development of a family structure possible. Today with increasing single parenthood, the family structure may be changing, but the sexual and reproductive imperative still exists to govern both temporary and long-term liaisons.

It is not difficult to imagine that for the survival of our species it would be in the interest of both men and women to see that their offspring thrive, and this was probably also as true in ancient times. A period when men were charged with the duties of hunting large game and women remained at home tending to the rigorous task of raising children. Rather than portraying this arrangement as a restrictive situation exploitive of women, it is possible to see it as an equitable division of labor that enabled both men and women to see their children grow and, in an evolutionary sense, to see their genes passed on. However, what we see as equitable, and related to our belief in sexual equality had to begin with a physiologic hormonal mechanism that brought the two sexes together. Again, it is our feeling that bonding has to be greater than the act of coitus alone for a family structure and child rearing to be effective. Although startling to some, oral sex, buoyed by pheromones, can be a catalyst to sustain relationships beyond the up and down of a seven-minute coitus.

Today, sexual attraction certainly does not rely on prolonged vaginal labial swelling (which would act as an air wick for the dissemination of attractive pheromonal scents) and visual arousal. Instead, both men and women dress or reveal skin and anoint themselves with perfume and cologne to entice members of the opposite sex. Atavistically, this obviously remains a part of our increasingly sexually overt culture, as seen in perfume sales, cosmetics and in sexually explicit magazines or pornography on the Internet, that still reflect on the physical or visual sensitivity of our primate ancestry. In evolution nature does not always eliminate the biochemical or physiologic pathways of past millennia; instead it co-opts and modifies the past, but the ancient physiologic pathway can still be recalled. This atavistic stimuli is best observed in pornographic films or in the response of viewers in a go-go bar. However, we should not look at the above behavior as the primary cause of changing mores regarding oral sex. This behavior has a long evolutionary history that transcends the availability of its popular cinematic expression.

Monkey behavior

As humans, we most closely resemble apes and our relationship to them may go back in evolutionary time some 2 million years. The estimated divergence from a common primate ancestor is thought to be approximately seven million years; humanoid apes may have existed for at least four million years. We can now measure heredity relationships using contemporary DNA techniques. These allow us to establish with authority the differences and similarities between primates or our monkey relatives.

To repeat, we differ from our closest evolutionary relative, the chimpanzee, by merely 1.6% of our DNA. The estimated time of species divergence among the apes is thought to be approximately seven million years. We differ from gorillas, genetically, by only two to three percent, and from monkeys by seven percent. The great similarity in the sequences of our DNA to that of the monkeys, chimpanzees, and the other great apes warrants a comparative review of monkey or primate sexual behavior, which may give insight into our own.

The role of sexual odor in monkeys has been widely studied (Michael, 1969; Michael & Keveang, 1968, 1971; Keveang, 1976). We know for example, a male rhesus monkey, when paired simultaneously with two females, will show a definite preference for one of them. This preference seems to be determined by their ovaries, which produce estrogen, the female hormone. Male preference (Evritt & Herbert, 1969), which in turn stimulates the female's pheromonal production, provides a "breeder" reactor-like effect. The ovarian-governed hormonal cycling, which controls the secretory function of vaginal mucosa and sweat or sebaceous glands in females, stimulates the male Rhesus monkey. Male grooming of female rhesus monkeys is also conditioned by their ovarian cycle; "flea-picking" (grooming) increases proportionately to pheromonal production based on vaginal secretion. Application of estrogenically stimulated vaginal secretions to non-ovulating females makes them attractive to the male Rhesus (Keverne & Michael, 1971).

"Copulins," as described previously, are the product of vaginal fatty acids produced by bacterial action on vaginal secretions (Bonsall & Michael, 1980). Vaginal copulins have been found both in the great apes and humans, but results are variable as to the consistency of their fatty acid composition (Fox, 1979) which varies with menstrual cycle and species. Fox (1982) feels that chimpanzee copulins may act as a primer odor stimulating frenzied male interest and copulatory behavior. Human copulin related odors are consciously palpable to both sexes during intercourse, and copulins have a subconscious sexually stimulating pheromonal effect, which explains both private and group sex-related release of inhibitions.

Date Rape

In most primates, odor is the critical attractive stimulus for the male. Increased levels of estrogen in females produces a more enthusiastic masculine interest when applied vaginally than when given orally as a hormone pill (i.e. in birth control) or by systemic injection. The anatomic presence of enhanced vaginal secretions is more pertinent to stimulating male interest than are overt female behavioral changes. What this means is that overall, a female rhesus monkey's behavior is less critical to male sexual interest than the quality of her vaginal odor (Michael, 1969). This is confirmed by experiments wherein plugging the nose of the male Rhesus abolished his sexual interest in nearby females.

We feel this behavior of the male rhesus may indeed be relevant to human behavior because it signifies that a male monkey's needs show less interest in a female's sexual desire or motivation than their own gratification. To the rhesus, smell is more stimulating than other patterns of response. Does this mean that men, like the rhesus monkey may, on occasion, be responding at a subliminal level to a woman's sexual odors, regardless of her other attractive features? Are we humans attracted sexually to each other based less on behavior or looks unless it is combined with the right endogenous scent?

While we are not monkeys, it's highly probable that the odor stimulus of the women men hold close can stimulate their sexual overtures. Although no one has, if we look, it is most likely that we will find that the initial sexual interest of a man or woman can be inhibited when we are suffering from an allergy or a stuffed nose.

This implies that the sexual motivation or emotional state of a woman at a particular moment can be almost irrelevant to male response if she is emitting a positive pheromonal signal. Whether a woman wants to participate or not, or whether she is sexually passive or aggressive may not be as critical to her would-be partner as compared to what her chemical message conveys to make her sexually attractive. As discussed previously, women must be "juicy" to be appealing to men. *Mouille*, vaginal moisture clinging to skin or undergarments provides a clear signal of a woman's sexual stimulation.

Obviously discordant pheromonal "messages" can cause problems. "Date rape" has become almost a politically correct definition for masculine aggression within the confines of an approved, polite, "boy meets girl, boy dates girl" social situation. What most frequently starts out as friendly interlude winds up with the "boy friend" forcing his sexual attention on his companion regardless of her efforts at refusal. If kissing occurs, touch and sexual excitement can lead to the production of vaginal moisture. Behavior based on pheromonal or vaginal copulin-related odors can then produce reactions that go beyond the politically or sexually approved behavior as outlined in the college manuals. Sexual intercourse or copulation, with its social restrictions, religious constraints and fear of pregnancy and disease are quite distinct from sexual arousal that expresses interest which does not necessarily mean commitment.

"Date rape" may thus have a physiologic explanation, as woman's subtle sexual odors act as a vomeronasal language beyond rational thinking that can elicit male sexual aggressiveness frequently, quite independent of her verbal objections or negative body language. While we are not in the least condoning the boorish behavior of selfish men made more boorish by unrestrained desire, we need to understand how copulins may contribute to this type of grossly inappropriate behavior.

According to some estimates, "date rape" or its attempt, has been experienced by 10 to 25% of college coeds, according to some surveys. What explains this high incidence? One explanation is that if female pheromonal output exceeds a threshold, it may trigger asocial behavior in pheromonal recipient males when his rational brain, that ordinarily exercises social restraint, is cortically suppressed by alcohol. Alcohol or drugs that weaken conscious control readily diminish our control of our libido. "Date rape" can also be a shared responsibility: a woman equally under the influence can welcome sexual stimulation that releases the moisture that radiates a pheromonal signal that produces the loss of rationality in both her and her male companion.

Trial lawyers who now attempt to defend overly aggressive males by blaming the aggrieved woman for wearing provocative apparel may find this to be less relevant than her production of provocative endogenous pheromones. While rape of any kind is a heinous crime, the fact that it exists may have less to do with male chauvinism, seeing women as the "weaker sex" and more to do with the primitive control of the male libido once rational social suppression is gone. A woman's pheromones can release in the male the crude beast that has been under increased control through four million years of evolution that has separated us from our ape-like ancestors.

Chapter 5

*"DON"T YOU SEE? She's clouded your mind! She's infected us
with some kind of pheromone extract!"*
— Batman (George Clooney) to Robin (Chris O'Donnell)

"A good nose is requisite to smell out work for the other senses."
— The Winter's Tale, Shakespeare

Acting like the animals we are

To recapitulate, our awareness of the importance of pheromones and
sexual odors has been overshadowed by our reliance on visual sexual
stimuli and by a desire to see ourselves as different from our animal
cousins. And so, when we are sexually attracted to someone, we comment
on anything but the real instinctual focus of our interest. Our courtship
mode – teasing, flirting, and touching in choreographed interactions
conceal the primitive nature of attraction, which are both a response to
and a demonstration of our pheromones in action.

We only need to observe our pets, such as our dogs, to see that much of
their behavior is driven by instinctual drives: the drive to hunt, to fight
other dogs, to mate, to have their ears rubbed or to chase cats. We
experience something very similar, albeit disguised beneath elaborate
socially conditioned behavior. We believe that when it comes to sexual
attraction, our rational, thinking mind is turned off and we are capable of
behaving in a manner that is not much different than that seen in our
randy dogs. There are similarities!

Because of our rational mind and our religious convictions, we are
embarrassed by our uncontrolled behavior, which is frequently irrational,
and unclean in that it puts us at risk for disease, that hurts not only our
self-interest, but our progeny and also those who love us. We see this in
illicit sex, recourse to prostitution, and in the behavior or those who are
ordinarily models of praise outside the sexual sphere.

Pheromonal communication

As explained in our first chapter, pheromones are created from hormone
secretions or stimulated by them. Once produced, fired, and detected,
pheromones are powerful messengers of sexual interest that are exchanged
between two people. Sexual odors stimulate the libido, even as the promise

and need of food can bring on hunger. The importance of sexually mediated odors in our lives goes substantially beyond the immediate selection of the one we love. Our romantic affinities, governed by desire and emotional bonding, provide for the survival of the species. The problem in understanding the importance of our sexual odors that influence our sexual behavior is partly because of the elusive nature of scent. This failure to acknowledge the significance of pheromones in our lives rests largely on the fact that our response to these odors is at least, initially, largely subconscious.

Rejection of pheromones, as a factor in human sexuality, is as absurd as separating the role of odor from our desire for food. Sexual odor is our subconscious companion rarely admitted in our society as a conscious part of our lives. Our reluctance to recognize sexual odors is a function of our social and cultural conditioning: Awareness of sexual odors is basically blocked by either psychological or social repression. Humans distinguish themselves from other mammals, such as cats, dogs, pigs, and horses, by largely denying or suppressing our awareness of sexual odors, even though a pheromonal evolutionary heritage is a part of our psyche. As humans our nose can recognize odor dilution in the atmosphere of 0.000,000,000,000,071 of an ounce. This has been described as like finding a friend in a football stadium. As mentioned earlier, perfumers can distinguish the origins of up to two to three thousand ingredients in a perfume bottle.

While supporting a multi-billion dollar perfume industry, paradoxically we have largely labeled preoccupation with sexual odors as "perversion" and relegated its discussion to titillating literature or pornography. We believe that this attitude will change as the chemical identification and characterization of human pheromones or copulins becomes better understood and their physiological or psychological effects can be directly tested. The search for human sexual attractants should now provide us with a rationale for scientific reappraisal of the role of pheromones in human gender identity and sexual behavior.

How we produce pheromones
Where do all these hormones or compounds come from that eventually produce pheromones? We believe that the production of pheromones begins with the natural production of steroid hormones like DHEA

(dehydroepiandrosterone) from pregnenalone, leading to the production of the male hormone testosterone (also present in lower concentrations in women) and the production of the predominantly female hormone, estrogen. Two other hormones, *androestendiol* and *androestentriol* are made by both sexes from the action of these precursor hormones on our skin. Experts tell us, however, that because sexually motivating hormones are largely made from DHEA, the "mother of all sexual steroid hormones," DHEA, in a sense, is the "raw material" that supplies pheromones in both men and women. As the parent hormone, DHEA, or its precursor, pregnenalone is essentially the same for each sex. Again, these hormones are predominantly produced by the brain and are called "neurocrines." During fetal development, the brain and skin begin their growth derived from stem cells, and both the skin and brain influence each other through the production of DHEA and its steroid metabolites.

"The male/female pheromones are the same," says Dr. Peter P. Pugliese, a dermatologist who is a consultant to companies that manufacture pheromone-related products. This is because "both males and females produce the same auxiliary chemicals that serve as pheromones," Dr. Pugliese says. In this way, he believes technically "there is no specific male (only) pheromone, or female pheromone in humans."

Dr. Pugliese believes DHEA production, which declines with age, is the key hormone involved in the production of pheromones. DHEA production tends to peak at the age of 25 and declines thereafter. In recent years, DHEA has received a lot of attention in the media as the elusive "elixir of youth," and to some degree, there is something to this. Our bodies naturally produce DHEA and rely on it for our ability to develop lean muscle tissue and maintain bone and skin youthful integrity. DHEA is the primary source from which our sex hormones are created and it has a great influence on our mental, reproductive, and sexual health, as well as resistance to infection. DHEA has been used in Europe as "prasterone" for 20 years to treat menopausal symptoms.

DHEA's role is demonstrated in the ordinary process of aging whereby DHEA levels decline in a linear fashion, so that in our 80s, we are producing only 15 percent of the levels of DHEA we made in our 20s. DHEA has been shown to have value in reducing stress injury, fighting depression, preventing carcinogenesis, and athersclerosis. As a hormone, it serves to enhance resistance against viral, protozoal and bacterial infection. DHEA also combats depression and in mice has been shown to enhance memory.

Pheromones in motion

Again, we recognize pheromones in action: couples sitting together, talking quietly, apart from the crowd. Progressing further, lovers are nuzzling each other's hair, with their noses not far from foreheads or underarms, which are sites capable of secreting pheromones. But what is happening between a couple that allows this to occur?

To review, sex hormones or their chemical precursors provide the basic materials for pheromone production. Our skin produces pheromones from the armpits, genitals, and also on the face –particularly the area between the base of the nose and the upper lip. Our skin plays a large role in allowing pheromones to become airborne to do their work. Our body hairs can act as wicks to release pheromones or to bind them for long-term presence on our surface. Any man with a moustache who engages in oral sex can evoke the memory of the experience when afterwards he strokes the hairs of his moustache. With fingers touching our genitals, we sample sexual odors that can linger on our skin and we can relive the erotic smells of our lovers and use their residual odors to stimulate our libido.

To repeat our initial discussion in our introductory chapter: the largest organ of the body, the skin has two types of glands that contribute to the production and distribution of pheromones: sebaceous and eccrine glands. "Sebaceous" frequently refers to all the secretory glands of the skin that provide lubrication. Sebaceous glands, "oil glands", generally are found on the genitals and nipples and in the groin and armpits where they produce secretions that are the origin of what is commonly known as one's body odor. One's "signature smell" results primarily from secretions from apocrine, or sweat glands where bacteria normally found living on the skin break down these secretions.

With age and loss of sexual hormones, dryness of skin becomes a problem. For many postmenopausal women, vaginal dryness becomes a problem. In women, the vaginal lubricating glands and Bartholin gland secretions are a key to pheromonal production that results in both subtle attraction and copulin production, the latter as discussed, can be a key element in date rape.

Unlike other pheromones, we are sensually aware of copulins and it is this odor-related, direct vaginal or penile lubrication that as genital-focused, identify without question our readiness for sexual intercourse.

Eccrine, or sweat glands distinct from sepaceous or apocrine glands, produce a watery, initially odor-free perspiration that travels to the skin's surface that will evaporate and keep us cool and prevent us from overheating. Sweat may dissolve or help make pheromones soluble to aid in their dissemination from our skin or apocrine glands.

Again, apocrine or sebaceous glands can be found all over the body but especially the ears, scalp, forehead, and genitals where they produce an oily substance on which bacteria can thrive. Bacteria also act directly on the skin cells that we shed each day from friction, sweat, or bathing.

An interesting fact to consider: one square inch of skin contains an average of 625 sweat glands, 90 sebaceous (oil) glands, 65 hair follicles, 20,000 sensory cells, and 24 feet of blood vessels. Do not forget the blood vessels, these are mainly skin capillaries, which provide the body with the dissemination of heat that makes our sexual odors volatile. With age our skin capillaries decline: blood vessels to the skin are under sexual hormonal control and our skin vascularity decreases with progressive age, along with menopause or climacteric decline.

Blushing or flushing red are examples of what we are talking about and this also relates to the tumescence, the swelling of the penis and vagina with arousal. This enhanced vascularization is not only designed for friction or penetration, but it disseminates pheromones that aid in enhancing our sexual responses. Flushing of non-genital skin, blushing, is not uncommon with sexual arousal.

In summary, the essence of sexual youthfulness is to be, literally, "juicy." All these glands produce their assorted secretions, which, in turn, are distributed on genitals, hair, and skin and mix with the bacteria that normally live on these areas. The curtain rises as pheromones are produced by our skin and ferried out to the world along with the millions of skin cells we shed daily. In an hour, we are capable of shedding more than six thousand skin cells per square inch of skin; this rapid sloughing of skin protects the body against bacteria. Alternatively, pheromones are released by volatiles mingled with the evaporation of our perspiration from hair and skin, or from genital lubrication. In a nutshell, that is how pheromones are produced, emitted and transmitted from one person to another.

Again, as discussed earlier, not all scientists will agree with the importance of pheromones to our sexual responsiveness. However, it is important to note that despite the debate that continues surrounding the nature of pheromones and the exact mechanism by which our bodies produce them, we respond to them! It is clear that they do exist! Ordinarily, pheromones at the onset are essentially odorless: it is only when the body's secretions mix with bacteria on the skin, that there is any obvious odor.

It is known that women tend to have a more acute sense of smell and interestingly, both sexes can identify the undergarments of those they are close to in both children and lovers. The main source of these odors are in the apocrine glands found in our armpits and that produce the oily secretions of our hair follicles that becomes a cosmetic problem with the development of acne.

Androstenol is a skin metabolite, derived from DHEA and our sex steroids, that has been shown to encourage women to linger when this hormone is applied to chairs in waiting rooms. It can also elicit a woman's interest in the opposite sex. Androstenol structurally is very similar to "boar scent," the odor found in the saliva of a male pig that sexually arouses the female pig for mating.

In contrast to the usual subtle odor of pheromones, indeed, under laboratory conditions, when concentrations of pheromones are amplified many times greater than is normally found, they can emit a strong smell that overwhelms our subconscious awareness. Of importance to the above, depending on the origin and their chemical structure, these scents are perceived differently by men and pre-menopausal women. "The scent of a pheromone in high concentrations say, 100 to 1,000 times what is normally available, produces a very unpleasant odor, similar to a foul cheese-like aroma," says Dr. Pugliese. Pheromones normally are an odorless component of our bodily secretions. However, at very low concentrations these pheromones are a sexual attractant.

The action of pheromones socially transcends our awareness of odor where response to these odors can very well result in unsought compliments related to our clothes, figure, or personality. These positive reactions are stimulated not always by preceding visual attraction but by a pheromonal subconscious awareness. Our own pheromones may serve to make us aware of our sexuality or our innate attractiveness without our perceiving that we are sensually receiving them. Apart from our visual appearance, how we smell influences the attitudes of the people who perceive us, and how we view ourselves.

The Case for Copulins

By our definition, pheromones are a chemical secreted by one member of the species that is recognized by a fellow member and this may result in a response that is behavioral or endocrinological. The final common pathway engendered by hormones is reproductive, recreational, or conducive to familial bonding.

As mentioned previously, one class of pheromones are copulins, which are generally responsible in mammals for the immediate impulse to mate or copulate and whose presence can be readily perceived following sexual lubrication or intercourse. Copulins are manufactured in response to the detection of pheromonal sexual odors, visual stimulation, or following genital touching. As stated previously, copulin production provides vaginal or penile lubrication, what the French call *mouille*.

When sexually aroused vaginally, women produce mouille which is the equivalent in physical obviousness to a male's tumescence. We should be aware that in these secretions, glands on or near our genitals, in both sexes, induce this moisture, resulting in sexually induced odors that both lubricate and govern our attraction for one another.

The lure of mouille, or lubrication, cannot be understated. Vaginal sexually-stimulated secretions, or mouille (copulins), combined in a situation where alcohol or mind-altering drugs have been ingested can result in a man committing violent acts in response to that odor that result, as discussed earlier, in date rape. It is not difficult to imagine any number of scenarios in which a man under the influence of drugs or alcohol asserts himself aggressively to a woman who is putting out a pheromonal signal associated with the sexual act. At best, this example provides a cautionary tale and reminds us that, along with many other compelling factors, the power of copulins, can lead to acts of pleasure involving bonding or love, or to acts of violence resulting in rape.

Through a complex interplay of cultural, emotional, and physical factors, humans based on familial, genetic, and social factors, have an overarching impulse to procreate. And, despite the centuries of religious stricture that would have us curtail sexual activity unless it was purely for sanctioned reproductive purposes, humans respond to the pheromonal impulses that condition sexual desire most frequently driven by the pursuit of pleasure. In today's modern world, it is almost reassuring it's possible regardless of how much technology would remove from the overarching cycles of nature, the pull of sexual attraction and the urgency to engage in sexual activity as too persistent to ignore despite religious constraint. Despite our pride in our civilized control, we respond with passion to the needs of our gene pool governing species survival. It is part of our evolutionary and genetic heritage. The pleasure principle provides the stimulus that makes us frequently pursue a reproductive course: we cannot deny that it is essentially pleasure that gives energy behind the addictive "urge to merge."

Historically, what distinguishes humankind is our complex social organization that has led to industrialized civilization. One must ask if civilization depends on collective societal masking of our awareness of sexual odors? Has this olfactory repression helped to develop our complex intellectual and social structures? The answer is that we have had to repress dramatic behavioral responses to sexually mediated pheromonal signals, for if we didn't and always behaved like dogs responding to "heat" (sexual signals), it would be impossible to carry on ordered conversation, thinking or work. Civilization would be impossible if our sexuality and its related aggression were not confined.

Look how difficult it is for long-term couples to coordinate their sexual desires, which governs so much of irritability in marriage relationships.

How much more difficult would our lives be if adolescent crushes or, bedroom aggression or passion, would become a constant, uncontrolled refrain in the workplace governed by the vagaries of odor sensitivities or pheromonal release?

Again, considering our current preoccupation with sexual needs and interest in finding our sexual partners, at work and play, how much more distracted would our life be without strong control of the thresholds of our sexual arousal? How could we exist as civilized humans in the presence of the release of hormonally-mediated odors that urge one to copulate as a priority over all other activities? Significant odor repression thus is at the heart of the social organization of humankind!

In the absence of cultural conditioning our ethical religious constraints could very well melt away like a sand castle in the tide of pheromone-induced desire. Religious expression, and its moral constraints, defining good and evil, would vanish at the first scent that triggered libido, unless human evolutionary development had not led to our ability to largely control these impulses. Instead, odor repression in humans may be of significant force to not only control the dangers of inbreeding, but to dampen competing aggression for sexual partners. Odor repression, its accommodation and our tolerance of scents, have to be a significant factor in our living together in increasingly crowded environments.

It is of interest that in regard to sexual priorities the average American is said to be capable of spending up to "three hours and 51 minutes each day watching porno" that amounts to "$10 billion a year in media sex." If this is true, it is obvious that visual overt sex stimulation exceeds Hollywood, rock music, concert and museum going as our primary entertainment. Again, if a visual stimulus as seen in filmed sex play has achieved such dominant interest, what will happen to our behavior if technology makes available pheromones in conjunction with the visual sexual stimulation now available in magazines, television or on the internet?

We have to be socially concerned not only with our personal identification and response to our sexual odors, but what will happen when these odors become cosmetically identifiable and commercially available? Will the availability of commercial pheromonal products help us to further enjoy our own sexual relationships or will they contribute to hedonistic adventures that will threaten to disrupt our lives? As with all powerful new technology, once the genie is out of the bottle, it is the responsibility of those rubbing the lamp to be prepared to either enjoy or temper their pleasure.

James Lewton Brian, in his book, *The Last Taboo*, states "our panhuman problem has always been, and no doubt will be, how these desires (sexual) can be met without interrupting other aspects of human society." As an example of cultural awareness, it is interesting to speculate on the fact that traditional Arab cultures seek to keep women veiled and at a distance to avoid men from being overstimulated by their presence or appearance. *Purdah* is an effective odor barrier as well as a visual barrier. Women in fundamentalist Afghanistan must veil both their faces and bodies to avoid tempting men.

In Orthodox Judaism and other religions, women, until recently, have been segregated or kept away from the altar of worship. "How can you think of God and your sins if pheromones, perfume, or sexual adornment distract you?"

In probing the value of psychic pain, Randolph Ness speaks to the value of anxiety and jealousy as factors motivating human responses. He speaks to the role of social obligations, adherence to rules as projecting long-term advantages over short-term gains. *"People usually forego ephemeral gains to avoid risking relationships, thanks in large part to anxiety that arises out of guilt or fear of punishment. Anxiety is aroused by socially unacceptable unconscious wishes."* The identification of human pheromones provides us with a new stimulus for anxiety, guilt, pleasure, and highly motivated behavior.

It seems obvious that sensitivity to sexual odors must be repressed within a social framework to manage the aggression, jealousy, and competitive disharmony that it can engender. Although as humans, we survive amid a hierarchy of power and odors that we see in the workplace, schools, and on the playgrounds, how much more difficult would life be if our sexual competition reduced us to the behavior of stags or bull seals competing aggressively for their mates each spring?

Incest taboo

As part of our definition of civilized behavior, we find that incest is forbidden in almost all societies. How did this come about? What governs this as an almost universally forbidden sexual act that makes good genetic sense. It has been observed that among children raised on an Israeli kibbutz, where all children share their lives, in a close family setting, that as children mature, although unrelated genetically, they seek sexual partners outside the bounds of their own kibbutz.

Why do Hutterites, as a closely inbred religious population, instinctively avoid marrying those with similar immunologic identity? Do close familial ties stifle sexual interest? Is it possible that the rarity of incest behavior in our culture is based on pheromonal differences that distinguish family from non-family members?

In explanation for the above, pheromones produce highly specific chemical behaviors in all animals ranging from insects to dogs. E. O. Wilson cites Roelof and Comery who described in 1969 two closely related species of moths whose female sex attractants differ by a single molecule. The male responds to his own species but is turned off by the molecular configuration of the closest related species though the chemical differences are hardly noticeable.

Long-term, familiarity with the odor of mother and father or their offspring may be too chemically similar for social behavior based on pheromonal stimulation for sex to occur. The long-term familial association with these odors might turn off any sexual interest, but instead enhances a supportive relationship that permits asexual social bonding between family members. This may represent a successful evolutionary adaptation preventing the deleterious effects of inbreeding and promoting the survival of healthy genes.

Looking for a different set of genes

People tend to select partners that "smell good" to them. Even in the case of a brother and sister being separated and raised apart, if they were to meet later in life, they are not likely to become sexual partners as they would not be likely to find each other appealing. Why is this so? It has to do with something called histocompatibility factor that governs successful organ and skin transplantation. People with similar genes can donate organs, skin, and blood to each other, but sexually are more apt to choose others who have a different genetic makeup, thereby increasing the chances their offspring will not be born with abnormalities.

From a strictly evolutionary standpoint the above makes sense: in order to increase one's chances for producing healthy children, it is critical to select a reproductive partner with a different set of genes than your own. What makes this possible is that we are able in some way to detect the proteins and peptides that provide a particular histocompatibility factor, in similar fashion to blood typing. Our nose acts like a blood-typing laboratory: one is likely to find the smell of a person with a dissimilar gene pool to be more appealing.

In an oft-cited study conducted by Swiss zoologist, Claus Wedekind, at Bern University, women sniffed the smelly t-shirts of men who wore them for an extended period of time. Both the men and women had their blood samples gene-typed for MHC antigens (major histocompatibility complex) involved in successful graft matching. Women preferred the t-shirts worn by men who were most dissimilar to them in terms of blood gene (MHC) type. Nature, in a sense, has helped us to instinctively "sniff out" potential mates that are from a different gene pool, thereby protecting us from bearing children with defects or wasting resources by birthing stillborn or damaged fetuses who are created from two sets of closely related genes that contain matching defects. In recent years, there have also been studies that suggest that men and women who have dissimilar gene types tend to be more fertile than those that are more alike.

The earliest bonds

Again, recent work has shown that five- to eight-month-old infants, apart from being aware of their mothers' breast or nipple odors related to nursing, show a sex difference in distinguishing a battery of test odors. At this early age, girls are more sensitive than boys to odor and while there is little difference in odor preference between the sexes in children aged three to five, there are gender differences that can be developmentally important in the long run.

The Freudian Oedipal concept of childhood preference for the mother can now also be seen as logically conditioned by pheromonal stimuli produced by maternal breast and body odor. Similarly, paternal odors may serve to strengthen male identity and condition female preference.

Moreover, the skin of the infant generates pleasant odors that establish its identity and helps to induce a loving bond with the mother, father, or grandparent. We believe that these infantile pheromones are important to the male parenting investment (MPI), which provide clues that govern a male's interest in his progeny.

Again, skin-generated odors of pilosebaceous origin (the oil glands of hair, skin, and sex organs) are distinctly different in male and female. It is possible that this is not just the result of glandular secretion controlling volatiles or the layers that flake or wash off our bodies: skin flakes contain histocompatibility proteins involved in the determination of organ transplantation that can influence odor production.

As examples: salivary glands are secreting organs that differ distinctly in rats between males and females in the ratio of mucous to digestive enzyme production. Although we have not established the nature of all the salivary differences between men and women, it is likely there is some mechanism by which we are attracted to the taste or smell of the breath or of the saliva of the sex that interests us, that may be a factor in our universal interest in kissing.

Smell and taste are anatomically not far removed from each other. In addition, our breath contains volatiles that reflect on our metabolic integrity. There are studies which show that chemical patterns in our expired air differ as to sex and age when analyzed by mass spectrophotography or peptide chemical determination. Is the breath of our loved one truly "sweet" or is this a pheromonal induced illusion related to love which can be seen as determined by the result of a chemical addiction related to pheromones?

It is our theory that pheromonal stimuli produced in skin, hair, breath, saliva, breast, and genitals occur in a developmental sequence governing the social behavior and sexual preference of children. This is particularly true when they leave their mother's breast and interact with their peers. All this becomes more important with the onset of adolescence.

The psychoanalytic emphasis is on oral fixation with emphasis on the breast as a source of nourishment. Nipple mouthing and the impact of its denial take on new meaning if odor guides the response. Nursing, which has been seen only as a question of oral gratification, provides an obvious environment for odor gratification as well. Bottle-feeding or the pacifier, and the absence of cuddling may result in pheromonal deprivation unless cuddling and kissing compensates for bottle-feeding as a substitute for the breast.

Recent work has shown that the bonding of lambs to their mothers, which is odor mediated, is triggered by the process of birth itself. Before delivery, the mother is immune to the odor of the lamb. However, immediately after delivery the ewe is attracted to the smell of the amniotic fluid, (the fluid component of the afterbirth), and within minutes she begins to smell, lick and sniff her newborn, and aid in its suckling. This event is triggered by a specific, immediate, postpartum response in the brain that turns on olfactory sensitivity to sensory clues provided by the newborn beginning with its birth odor. What this says is that brain centers can be conditioned by physiologic or endocrine events that rapidly turns on odor awareness almost instantly, responsible for bonding and mothering!

Immature female rats are repelled by mature male odors, but with maturity, they are attracted to them. Extrapolating from birthing sheep, what we are saying is that we humans are amazingly like sheep, in that our brain centers can be turned on by hormones or environment-mediated events which affect our subconscious odor awareness, resulting in profound behavioral social responses. For example, parenting or grandparenting is associated with instant love when we see or hold the newborn child or grandchild. It is clearly a composite process based upon our view of the helpless infant, its cry, its warmth, and its odor.

The family

Our emphasis on pheromone influences governing sexual behavior and bonding between parent and child, as well as possibly influencing aggressive behavior, requires that we evaluate odor as a factor in the origin of the human family and its social structure.

Western society, in the Judeo-Christian tradition, is monogamous and heterosexual in its structure, but in turn, we cope with divorce as legitimized serial polygamy, and the existence of small but significant homosexual and bisexual relationships. Of 1,154 past and present societies on earth, 980 practice or practiced polygamy. What governs these differences, and can pheromones have exerted an evolutionary effect on what we see as Biblical truth?

Monogamy can be defined "as a permanent union of male and female for the fulfillment of sexual function." Of practical concern to our own society, monogamous males and females share parental duties. "Monogamous fathers take more care of their young ones than do polygamous fathers." (Alsverdes, 1935; Dewsbury, 1987)

Among the primates, only the lesser primate gibbons are monogamous. In gibbons, it has been observed that the male sex drive, as compared to other primates, is "low" but despite a defined estrus period in the female gibbon, copulation outside of estrus can occur as in humans, outside the period of ovulation thus removing copulation from estrus. As in humans, "heat," or estrus defining the availability of a fertile egg, is not absolutely necessary for this primate's sexual interaction, but effectively defines the monogamous state of the gibbon which as in humans is their devoted shared parentage.

Searching for an understanding of human bonding, it is of interest that Dewbury, in a biological appraisal of monogamy, presented exceptions to the concept that shared parenting is always related to its origin at conception. This is seen in the female rodent, the Mongolian gerbil, who territorially bonds to a single male, but with estrus, pursues foreign males, only to return to her territorial base and the original male's territory after estrus ends and pregnancy begins. The key fact is not male impregnation, but territoriality defining a shared nesting place. Obviously, exclusivity in mating or paternity is not always necessary for family structure if pheromones are involved.

The best example of a possible pheromonal determinant for monogamy is seen in the prairie vole. This rodent species, found in our western states, is divided into subspecies that are studied for their marked differences in sexual behavior. The mating behavior of voles is based on odor perception. Faced with the option for mating with four estrus females, the male prairie vole prefers to select one; while the mountain vole will copulate with all four.

The female prairie vole also prefers a familiar mate. What designates this familiarity that leads to copulation is odor perception?

Prairie vole males spend more time with single females in contrast to other vole subspecies such as mountain or meadow voles. While frequency of copulation is less in monogamous voles, intromission is much longer than in the polygamous subspecies. Monogamous prairie voles copulate with more thrusts per intromission and fewer mounts before ejaculation. In contrast to other vole subspecies, sexual behavior was less frequent in the monogamous prairie vole, but sexual interaction and male to female time together is longer. Monogamous prairie vole males do not prefer strange females and spend more time copulating with the one they have selected.

The prairie vole male prefers unmated females to those that have been mounted by another male. Again, monogamous prairie voles spend more time in sexual intercourse. While we humans resemble prairie voles, we must ask if monogamy and pheromonal interest enhance the pleasure of sexuality to extend its enjoyment? This suggests that apart from pheromones we must look at other hormones like oxytocin, a peptide hormone, that in addition to stimulating uterine contraction, or the release of milk, stimulates a desire for cuddling, and close body contact, in animal models. Do pheromones prompt the release of oxytocin? Do pheromones extend the pleasure of sexual intercourse? Oxytocin is released during orgasm and in rodents is responsible for cuddling.

Are humans more like prairie or mountain voles? From our behavior and social structure, we appear to be more like prairie voles, but are certainly not absolute in our monogamous character.

The Family: Darwinian, Marxist, or Pheromonal Factors at Work?

Views as to the origins of human social structure have been controversial. In opinion, they range from a Marxist economic focus to a heredity-related emphasis as to the role of Darwinian evolution or sociobiology. Our view is primarily Darwinian, as we think that evolution and its adaptive role could have given rise to human social structures as they exist today. The best presentation of this position is that of Robert Wright in his recent text, *The Moral Animal* (Pantheon, N.Y., 1994).

In contrast, Lila Leibowitz in her text, *Females, Males, Families* (Duxbury Press, N. Scituate, Mass., 1978) presents the argument that the development of nuclear families is based on social pressures governed by the exchange of goods and services. While Liebowitz gives emphasis to the remarkable variety of family structure seen in worldwide ethnic or social differences in both humans and apes, her focus with humans is primarily economic. She ignores pheromones or limerance (joy) as factors in family cohesion.

Historically, we feel that the evidence supports that the human family developed under social circumstances strongly related to the environmental factors governing food availability. The influence of religious and governmental control of family structure provides cultural extensions reinforcing the necessary economic bonds that hold family groups together. The family's function is to maintain nutrition and shelter and with children, to nurture the continuance of the species.

Evolutionary theory hold that humans developed in a hunter-gatherer society similar to that found in baboon colonies or as is seen in the vanishing African Kung Bushman society. As in baboon society, human males are the more muscular sex. Unencumbered by child bearing and nurturing, men became the hunters that were free to wander long distances to obtain fish or game, while women remained at home to look after the children and forage locally for food.

Leibowitz feels that labor, as divided in human society, is not necessarily correlated with the biologic or physical attributes of the sexes. "Once a division of labor along sex lines becomes established, men and women are forced into mutual dependency where the minimum viable economic unit capable of sustaining itself becomes one that includes one male and one female."

Based on her interpretation of human behavior, Leibowitz believes that sexuality is not a key factor in sustained human bonding. Her evaluation of female sexuality ignores the place of Stoddard's "hidden estrus" as a factor providing women with control of their own sexuality. She ignores the fact that sex, as a reward, can easily persuade men into sustaining long-term relationships. This would be particularly true if there were a scarcity of men or women that would require the incentive of sex to strengthen any economic exchange of food or services where sex would serve to bring people together. In that sense, a woman's control of her sexuality can be a commodity for economic exchange. However, in contrast to Leibowitz's position, it is our feeling that although humans are culturally plastic, the availability of sexual partners and sexual experience is as important to the formation of family or social structure, as that governed by the availability of food and shelter.

Particularly when there are no scarcities, other factors are critical. As seen in our society today, it is obvious that without shortages of food and shelter, sex can become the major preoccupation that binds us together. In view of the weakening of family structures and the serial polygamy of divorce involving 50% of us, does the loss of pheromonal appeal contribute to the divorce rate? With growing economic and social independence of women will pheromonal influences possibly predominate to bring us together or sunder familial relationships that ordinarily provide for our children? With age, we lose sex hormone production and its pheromonal response!

The control of sexuality as a concern of church and state is based on the need for stability in a society that requires firm ground rules to keep it functioning. There is an additional element in family structure associated with male aggression and possessiveness. This is a factor in human society that has to be given attention: Jealousy summarizes its effect on male behavior that has a sociobiologic explanation if one looks at animal behavior: In lions and certain monkey species, males kill the young sired by others. This puts the female once more into ovulation (heat); her pheromonal signal of availability then gives the male killer his opportunity to perpetuate his own genes over that of his predecessor.

In humans, with a female estrus hidden from the male spouse, male jealousy became a feature seeking to guard a spouse's ovaries from another male's poaching. Jealousy can be seen as an adaptive feature to perpetuate firm familial genetic identity, which biologically explains the development of harems, *purdah* and excuses for punishing adulterers among humans. All societies have found ways to cope with sexual jealousy as a factor in human behavior. If you are a possessive male, pheromones have to be kept under control to prevent loss of social control and to avoid another's encroachment on one's gene pool.

What is the difference between a Moslem sheik that controls four legitimate wives, and numerous concubines, and the financially successful Westerners that engage in multiple divorces or trophy wives? Men in our society are pheromonally sensitive and if wealthy or powerful, often seek to emulate the rutting stag. Alternatively, in our society power or deceit can add incentives to pheromonal attraction between the sexes. While religion serves to focus our attention on responsibility, as sexual beings wired to respond to our physiological non-familial promptings, we may often struggle to not succumb to the overwhelming desire to act on our sexual yearnings.

As we know, there are exceptions to family exclusivity as seen in the swingers of our own time and among certain adolescents with their rampant sexual behavior. This is a growing concern in our society, which contrasts with the authoritarian masculine or polygamous control of women in other societies. One can only contrast purdah in Moslem societies with bikini bottoms and coconut oil glistening on the rumps of Western women.

While the structure of families can be the result of cultural and economic history, we feel that the fundamental underlying key to family behavior that is closest to our species in consensual mating, grooming and broad family associations is seen in the primate bonobo chimpanzees or the rodent prairie vole. In human-like primate subspecies, sexual stimulation is a significant adhesive force governing procreation and survival and this is also observed in the rodent monogamous vole. If the bonobos can be seen as an example for the study of human evolutionary behavior, we must also understand that we are held together primarily by touch, vision and pheromones, which may release neuropeptides similar to oxytocin that encourages cuddling and can lead to orgasm. All this while appearing contrary, is necessary for parental responsibility and familial bonding to be established and maintained.

Regardless of social mores cultural differences between men and women are not immutable, but biologically we crave the opportunity for both stimulation and relaxation epitomized by the pleasures of sexuality. When these are denied or deficient, alternatives develop as seen in Victorian society where the denigration of women's sexuality resulted in an expansion of male participation in commercial prostitution.

In addition, it is of interest to us that neither Lebiowitz nor Michaels whose work is concerned with the origins of family structure make reference to sexually transmitted disease as a factor in the ascendancy of religious and governmental control of family structure. We see the significance of this today with the increase of AIDS, syphilis and other sexually transmitted diseases. The strengthening of fidelity as a rational approach to the threat of lethal and debilitating disease makes sense, as these sexually transmitted diseases destroy not only the individual, but progeny and entire societies. We are seeing the results of this with HIV infection in the sub-Sahara regions such as Uganda and South Africa, and where the threat in Thailand, India, and other Asian countries is quite evident. Thus, it is not only economics or pheromones that dictates familial structure but disease and fear of debility and death that re-enforces the appropriate hold that religion has on the social structure of our families.

Parenting requires that we hold and pet our children. "Love my dog, love me, or my children." To play with a puppy or kitten is an expression of a parental gene response. In old age homes, a pet dog or cat can show affection governed by touch and odor to those isolated by their age and/or lack of adequate family support. The reaction of our dog that licks our hand and wags its tail to our odor, describes in simple terms what parenting and family interaction and pheromones are all about.

Hopefully, our understanding of the above will improve with application of our awareness of our olfactory sensitivity which, in addition to touch, will serve to support those isolated because of age, divorce, familial loss or physical problems. We have to see our pets, cats and dogs, as both a stimulus and an example as to what is needed in human behavior to re-enforce our familial strength. Will the discovery of available pheromones serve to enhance bonding and prevent divorce or will it become a competitive distraction overwhelming our sensory and social interactions? This is of particular concern, as discussed earlier, as seen in our growing preoccupation with pornography.

We maintain that one anchor to family identity and male/female and child long-term interaction is based on the mutual supportive attraction of our odors. This pheromonal influence includes the attachment of men, and, of course, women to our offspring. To love a pet is a model for child love.

However, in addition to the above, we must be aware that sexual arousal is the link between reproduction and the life of the family and community. Genital stimulation plays an important role in the success of mammalian reproduction. In addition, it gives rise to pheromones, which are both rapid and slow mediators to the absolute strategy of human fertility. To erotically respond to pheromones, we need our nose with its specialized nerve receptors to make us reproductively successful, and to assure the viability of parenting and species survival. Sex is not only reproductive, but influences the quality of our lives!

Our sensitivity to the world around us is sensually greater than we imagined, and it is time that we looked at ourselves comparatively with those who share our domestic hearth, like the dogs and cats that astound or repel us with their sexual antics. Our pets are dominated by the influence of sexual odors, so that to civilize them to make their behavior domestically tolerable, we castrate them early in life. In relation to pheromonal response, human castration is not physical, but mental as in large measure we have lost social and conscious awareness of the importance of our own sexual odors. We are frequently pheromonally castrated. We suffer a psychological "nose bob" because of religious or cultural restraints!

It is our thesis, because of our increased awareness of the exquisite subconscious human sensitivity to pheromones that it can help us to understand both rational and seemingly irrational sexual behavior. Hopefully, this awareness will provide a strong alternative to a limited religious view of sex, whether Jewish, Christian, Muslim or of other religious origin, that see sexuality existing only as a reproductive phenomenon. This has robbed countless generations of their birthright as sex is designed, along with the pheromonal stimuli that accompanies it, to create long-term relationships between couples, thus providing for children and multi-generational families which demonstrate that sex has social value apart from its reproductive role. We feel that it is time that both religion and psychiatry recognize the place of pheromones in our personal and societal structures.

Chapter 6

"Since when it grows and smells, I swear,
Not of itself but thee."
— Ben Johnson

"The only way to get rid of a temptation is to yield to it."
— Oscar Wilde

"A little experience often upsets a lot of theory."
— Cadman

"I wear it everyday: it's a part of my morning ritual. It's
unbelievable. When I put it on, it gives you a mind-boggling
euphoria. I already have a lot of confidence to begin with, but
this basically enhances it. It gives me a thousand times more
confidence when I use it. . ."
— Robert, 74 – Boca Raton, Florida

"I can tell there's something going on. Normally when I wear
it, they come in and they want to chitchat. My ex-boyfriend
won't stop bothering me."
— Samantha, 35 – Portland, Oregon

"I'm usually really wary about guys in a bar. He was talking
about that special connection he had found across the room and
telling me he didn't know what it was, but I was special and he
had to make sure I knew it."
— Beth, 28 – Long Beach, Calif.

Love Potions

The world is full of legends regarding the effectiveness of spells to win the heart of the beloved, or to poison a rival that interferes with access to the beloved. To achieve success in love, in this manner, one has to have recourse to a witch doctor, or some authority that provides the successful, magic formula. Today, modern day witch doctors may very well be the perfumers who have incorporated the latest in pheromone research to provide their customers with a product that is truly bewitching. In this chapter we will examine how the commercial manufacture of pheromones has progressed from literally using pig pheromones, closely related pheromones, derived from the swine to those of human origin. Currently, while only a handful of companies offer pheromone-based products, as seen on the Internet or men's magazines, there is good reason to believe more will follow as testing and the media exposure creates more demand for these natural products, and women see value in their application.

We should also examine potential health benefits that might be derived from the use of pheromone-based products. While much more research needs to be conducted to provide more evidence of actual health benefits, in the case of pheromones, it may be that, like falling in love, the "Experience almost always surpasses the Theory". To this end, we will also hear from a number of people who have used pheromone-based products and learn about their experiences. Lastly, we will consider future applications for this cosmetic technology, as it is further refined and matures.

When we first began our examination of the role of odor in human sexuality, we wondered why clinically the personal awareness of pheromones appeared to be virtually absent in our culture. We first speculated that our inability to recognize odor as sexually important may have been based on evolutionary changes intrinsic to human origin. We felt that this inability to recognize odor as sexually important originated because it was required for the development of orderly civilized conduct between the opposite sexes. It is obvious that one couldn't maintain a functional society if men and women were to compulsively and aggressively chase after one another at the first whiff of a sexually attractive odor. Clearly, as seen in dogs and cats, pheromonal responses have the potential to disrupt social behavior.

We now feel that the repression of sexual odor was primarily influenced by cultural attitudes that have inhibited frank discussion, to say nothing of investigation in Western society. One has to ask if negative attitudes toward human pheromonal responses influence us culturally. We must ask, which came first, the repression of the awareness of sexual odors or the sociobiologic behavior that de-emphasized or penalized those that would make this a visible key feature of their human bonding and identity?

However, not all societies and cultures are so inhibited. As discussed in our introduction, Dawn Lamb, in collaboration with June Cleveland, in the late 1930s explored villages between Oaxaca and Chiapas, north of the Gulf of Tchuantepec, on the Pacific side of the Mexican jungles, where Mexican Indian culture discovered the important role scent played in the selection of sexual partners in this community.

Other cultures have also been aware of the importance of scent. The Fragrance Foundation of New York, lists the following customs as examples of how compelling human smell is in many cultures around the world:

The Burmese phrase for "Give me a kiss" is "Give me a smell." Borneans never "greet" anyone; they "smell" them. On the Gambia River in Western Africa, when a man greets a woman, instead of shaking hands, he puts the woman's hands to his nose and smells the back of them twice. The Chuckchee of Siberia greet each other by sniffing down the back of the neck. In one hill tribe of India, they sniff at a friend's cheek and say as a greeting, "Smell me!" And, a Mongol father shows his son affection by smelling him.

This obsession with smelling one another has continued to this day, and we believe that smell can amplify or quell sexual interest in a potential mate. In a survey conducted by the Fragrance Foundation to determine the importance of smell in contemporary sexual relationships on a scale from 1 to 10, women scored 8.5, and men, 7.5, indicating their feeling that odor had a positive influence on their sexual interest.

Manufacturing sex appeal

Throughout the ages, people have slathered their bodies with scented oils, burned incense, candles, and anointed themselves and one another for the ritual of worship and to pay homage to the one they love. Today, pheromones are available from multiple manufacturers, each claiming that it, exclusively, has a formula containing human-based pheromones. One has only to explore the Internet or pick up any men's magazine to find promotional material.

Not long ago, in the 1980s, when the discovery and media buzz surrounding pheromones was stimulated by the production of pheromone products based on "boar scent," boar salivary secretions that attract female pigs, many consumers felt hoodwinked as these products were created from animal-based pheromones, but were not derived from humans. The conventional wisdom sounded like a bad joke: "If you want to attract male pigs, wear their product – it's made from pig pheromones!" However, these pig steroid compounds do have clinical relevance to androsterone and related steroid structures found in sweat or saliva in human and mammalian physiology. David L. Berliner, M.D., who holds a patent (USP 5,278,141, 1994) speaks to the effects of 16-androstenes and estrenes, male and female hormones respectively, found in human skin, sebaceous secretions, and sweat which influence olfactory receptors in our vomeronasal organs, in a sex-determined way.

With continuing research being conducted, the new generation of pheromone products are a far cry from the early products based only on boar pheromones (boar scent.) Again, by our definition of pheromones, in order to be classified as such, these secretions are produced and detected by members of the same species, and, once detected, often result in a change in behavior related to effects that differ for each sex involved.

The pursuit of love, that "dark and doubtful presentiment" that draws lovers together has been given a scientific basis. The commercial application of pheromones is upon us. Most recently, Monti-Bloch and Grosser (1991) in a study supported by the REALM (formerly the Erox Corporation) have evaluated pheromonal responses by measuring electrical potentials generated directly from the vomeronasal organ. Pheromones derived from human secretions produce responses in a sexually dimorphic manner. Their coded pheromone perfume EA-830 stimulates men, while, in contrast, EA-670 produces a response in women. What these compounds are has not been revealed. But, pheromonal evaluation of the these compounds are not only subjectively reported, but clinical response is based on blood pressure, skin conductance, and even changes in human brain waves. With no overt odor awareness necessarily demonstrated in the subject, the stimulated subject responds physiologically, but may have no cognitive awareness of odor. These pheromones, isolated by Berliner's group may represent a pathway to our true sexual subconscious.

These subconscious responses are based on vomeronasal stimulation exclusively, as pheromonal compounds do not stimulate the main olfactory system (MOS) that is ordinarily what we use to identify the smells of food, plants, flowers, and excrement. Of particular interest to the sexual role of pheromones in humans is the specificity of the REALM pheromonal human response. For best results, we need human-derived compounds to get a response in humans. However, that is not entirely true as the odor of musk (derived from animal anal glands), has been a mainstay of perfumers for centuries.

There is also a sexually differentiated, focused heterosexual or homosexual sensitivity, depending on the pheromone administered. Only human-derived odors, as compared to animal-based pheromones, such as musk, produce the best responses.

Again, the ability to verbally label an odor governs our apparent capacity to identify it. However, among pheromone-related observations, where up to 50% of men do not smell androsterone (boar scent, the odor sexually stimulating to female pigs,) there is evidence of a subliminal physiologic awareness as human skin conductance changes occur to androsterone. This indicates an effect of the odor, despite our inability to describe it.

In human subjects, there exists unconscious odor conditioning which alter mood, attitude, and behavior. This has been reviewed by Kirk-Smith et al. (1983), who showed that to experience an unfamiliar odor under stress often conditions a future response. The authors observed that natural odors could acquire conditioning value without subjective awareness. These authors also feel that memory for initial odor association is long-lasting. Once one experiences an odor of emotional impact *a la Proust*, it remains with you for life and can influence your erotic fantasy.

Anatomically, this makes sense as vomeronasal responses are governed by their relationship possibly to terminal nerve and most importantly, on VOS-linked connections (vomeronasal sensitivity) ancillary olfactory bulb brain activity. The ancillary olfactory brain nucleus is distinct from the MOS (main olfactory system). In contrast to the main olfactory system, which responds to food odors, the vomeronasal neural pathways do not have major connections to the cortical (thinking) areas of the brain. Thus, again, vomeronasal induced memory is primarily subconscious, and although it produces striking behavioral responses, these are not necessarily cortically or consciously induced, but proceed from within the brain to effect behavior that we may have difficulty in explaining. Thus, though outraged, we should not be surprised by date-related rape when alcohol suborns rational thinking and the chemical pheromonal stimulus is present.

The subconscious place in our brain governing the awareness of sexual odors explains our inability to readily describe these odors as well as its irrational affect on our behavior. Again, it is of interest to find that with notable exceptions, most sexually explicit literature, particularly pornography, is relatively sparse in its references to the odors of sex. One is inundated with visual description, but our positive vocabulary for genital odors is limited. After "pungent," "flowery," "musky," and "overwhelming," "subtle," "funky," we are left with very little else. Despite the deficiencies of many authors in describing odors' sexual importance, a cogent minority have anticipated our current scientific interest with their own subjective observations that describe this important aspect of human sensory awareness.

We have an extremely active, successful perfume industry whose goal is not only to mask socially unpleasant odors, but to develop odors that are sexually attractive. It is of interest that Epple (1985) described a very human primate behavior that involved "mixing" (fingering) of odorous materials that were then self-applied to various parts of the monkey's body. Not unlike these monkeys, people have anointed themselves with colognes, perfumes, and scented oils in hopes of attracting others to them as well as for the general sense of well being they induce.

Among the handful of companies that offer products that they say are designed to enhance sexual attractiveness, confidence, and well being, as examples, we will mention three. The first is REALM (formerly known as Erox Corporation), which was founded by one of the pioneer researchers of pheromones, David Berliner, M.D., an anatomist who first worked with pheromones at the University of Utah in the 1960s. He noticed that during his research in the lab, when he left the uncovered vials containing what he learned many years later were pheromones, open, he noticed that the other researchers in the lab were more social and convivial towards one another. When he closed the vials, the researchers returned to their usual, less than collegial ways. Now, three decades later, Berliner has developed perfumes that "contain synthesized human pheromones as a component" that "have been shown to stimulate the human vomeronasal organ."

In 1990, the *New Scientist* reported the isolation of a steroid molecule from human sweat at the University of Warwick, UK, an observation similar to that of Berliner's. This led to a pheromone "Osmone I," and the creation of a company to market it. Unfortunately, this work is not updated in the scientific literature. These perfume companies depend on advertising and secrecy to survive, thus "Osmone I" is missing from our Medline database literature source.

At one time, the work of REALM might have sounded futuristic, because the company was trying to harness the power of pheromones for use in our daily lives. Their work is in commercial development to apply human pheromones the way we apply skin cream or perfume. The health benefits that REALM says its pheromone-related products impart, includes putting " you and your partner at ease, boosting your confidence, and enhancing romantic possibilities by contributing to your mutual feeling of well-being." Again, the manufacturer makes these claims, but as with all products on the market, the slogan for any smart shopper should be, "Buyer beware!"

Berliner's work was important, because he was among the first to recognize, in the late eighties, that as humans we possess a nasal receptor system (VOS) sensitive to human derived sexual odors. However, again, up until the last 15 years, it was felt by most physiologists that as humans, only 10% of us possessed the same pheromonal detector found in all other mammals. As discussed earlier, this debate continues and the VOS is still thought by many to be vestigial in humans. A shrinking group of olfactory neuroscientists still believe that pheromones are of no consequence to human sexual awareness. However, via microelectrode placement, and physiologic recordings, most humans are found to be no different in their sexual odor sensitivity than the dogs and cats whose behavior we deride.

The newfound awareness of pheromonal sensitivity has been commercially available as REALM markets their human sex stimulants as unique products with particular application to each sex. Other major players in the perfume and cosmetic industry have already introduced their own line of pheromone-related perfumes or like cosmetic giant, Estee Lauder, they are similarly hard at work identifying specific human pheromones.

Other company, such as the Athena Institute of Chester Springs, Pennsylvania, has also produced products they say are derived from human pheromones. Founded by research biologist Winnifred Cutler, Ph.D., who was responsible for the seminal work that led to the discovery of pheromones producing menstrual synchrony among women, Dr. Cutler has continued to conduct research on how pheromones affect us, and, in particular, how they relate to the reproductive health of women.

Lastly, Eroscent, manufactured by Health Freedom Nutrition, based in Santa Rosa, California, has also produced a pheromone-derived product that is universally available for both men and women. We will learn more about people's actual experiences with Eroscent later. Eroscent is placed on the upper lip so that its odor inputs directly into our nose to affect the VOS. Eroscent functions as a universal "pro-drug" to be metabolized by our nasal receptors to input our brain and to stimulate us to produce the pheromones that sexually identify us. It begins as a "unisex" stimulant, as the same product works for either sex, and we respond by releasing our own gender-determined pheromones in response to Eroscent impinging on our nasal VOS receptors.

Aromatherapy
Tisserand discusses the history and current knowledge of perfumes as therapeutic tools. The history of perfumes goes back to pre-biblical and biblical history. "Holy perfume" utilized frankincense and myrrh. To this day, incense and the aroma of spices are part of many religious rituals. Saints, despite death, are supposed to generate pleasant odors, instead of those of decay.

The Greek philosopher, Plutarch, wrote about an ancient Egyptian perfume known as kyphi. "It's aromatic substances lull to sleep, allay anxieties and brighten dreams. It is made of things that delight most in the night."

"Feeling good is a basic human need, and 'olfactory ecstasy' was discovered by human kind very early on," Tisserand says. He adds that it is difficult to distinguish between spiritual and sexual "highs" and he cites the long history of kyphi and of its ingredients, as an aphrodisiac, or even of its value in the treatment of asthma.

Aromatherapy is a modern approach to evaluating the effects of plant and flower-derived essential oils on physical, mental, and emotional responses. A discussion of the therapeutic application of essential oils as medicine deserves evaluation in a controlled modern medical university setting. Today, the use of aromatherapy is largely restricted to naturopathy and other alternative medicine practitioners. However, essential oils have been shown to be of value as sedatives, massage enhancers, anti-anxiety, or anti-depressants. Responses to these odors, like pheromones, are beyond conscious control, but induce changes in blood pressure, skin conductance, and brain waves that are reproducible.

Our awareness of sensitivity to pheromones can be seen as a response despite chemical odor dilutions in the remote range of parts per billion. If humans can react to their own pheromones without conscious awareness, then the rationale for aromatherapy requires serious consideration by modern medicine. Again, our olfactory system involves four separate cranial nerves, if we include the terminal nerve, within our nose, each carrying information to the most primitive centers of our brain. For this reason, it should not be surprising that aromatic substances can affect our moods, tension and attitudes with or without sexual arousal as a part of the experience.

What is more, aromatherapy is most frequently combined with baths, massage, or therapeutic touch. We need serious evaluation of aromatherapy, and can see it best applied with physical therapy and massage to which it has been allied over the centuries.

Tales of Pheromones

Much the way that aromatherapy and the use of essential oils is gaining more widespread use, so too, are pheromones, as more products are placed on the market and pheromone research continues to mature.

For many, the use of pheromone perfumes or their placement in perfumes or colognes appear to have increased social confidence, self esteem, and allowed users to put their best foot forward in communicating with their peers. This can also be true for upscale perfume provided by the perfumers and cosmetic companies like Estee Lauder, l'Oreal, etc. For others pheromones are sought for the specific claims made on behalf of its appeal to overt sexuality. The need to accelerate attractiveness between couples related to its action in leading in no uncertain terms to the desire to couple. Here we are dealing with the evolutionary drive that led to creation of pheromones in the animal kingdom. An end point in sexuality that is designed to separate our limbic brainstem from the rational thinking of our highly evolved cerebral cortex. In the latter case one can observe the ads that have populated Men's magazines over the past decade where there is no question as to the motives that have led to their creation.

In regard to pheromone action at the clinical level I have been involved with the development of Eroscent. This is a pheromone derived from our native human hormone Dehydroepiandrosterone. (DHEA). DHEA and its metabolites secreted by our skin decreases with progressive age and DHEA is present in both men and women. It gives rise to both testosterone and estrogen. A processed DHEA contained in Eroscent has been shown in a double blind study to enhance sexual attraction between both sexes.

Eroscent is applied by application to the upper lip directly beneath our nostrils to allow its scent to act directly on our vomeronasal receptors. However, its action may be applicable to wherever lovers place their noses in the search for intimacy.

Eroscent is unisexual in its appeal and we feel that its action is reciprocal between the sexes. Responding to it, with or without touch, we make our own pheromones to provide social exchange or to further attract and encourage our lovers.

What most users are looking for is described in the following experience of a 28 year old Eroscent user:

"There was a guy nearby and I happened to glance at him. He took that as his cue. He was acting as if he had in me the woman he wanted to spend the rest of his life with. He was talking about the special connection we had found across the room and telling me that there was something about me, he didn't know what it was, but I was special and he had to make sure I knew it. The pheromones certainly had an effect on him!"

Of course this can happen without Eroscent, and not all users are satisfied. One must ask if pheromones can restore the limbic attraction between elderly couples bound together in long term relationships? Can pheromonal attraction lend permanence and intimacy to lovers? Does it aid courtship or is it a placebo effect related to the creation of our belief in its activity? Is its action the equivilant of putting on an exiting garment; sharing a vacation; an exiting visit to the theater, or the dance? Is the pheromone Eroscent the equivilant of a full moon on a balmy spring evening? Or does it relate to when someone we are fond of or dependant on, rewards us with a compliment or a gift? Does it relate to the elation we get when we are triumphant or happy? Beyond its sexual role and its release when sensuously moved are pheromones also produced as a subconscious response to happiness or contentment? Do we release pheromones with the happiness we share in someone else's joy, or the aesthetics of a sunset, our love for a child, or the excitement of a football game? In that regard, is something telling us as we breathe it in, subconsciously now is the to reinforce our bonding, to share our love with others and to open ourselves to reproduction.

Buyer Beware

The purchase of pheromones should not always be based on its sexual message as it may also help by changing the way you interact with your family, coworkers, or in the social arena, attracting more attention than you may have previously been accustomed to. We must be aware that there are health, religious, and social implications to consider.

The availability of pheromones is not under FDA control to determine the genuineness of claims or the possibility of long-term biological or toxic side effects. Remember too that using a pheromone-based product may place you in the center of more attention from others than you have experienced before. It is important to be aware that pheromonal communication is what you see driving the sexual behavior of your dog or cat. At another level it can influence maternal response as aside from the overt sexual nature of pheromonal communication, we believe the intimate bonding that occurs between lovers can also be seen between parent and child within one's family. We believe pheromones govern the final act of eroticism, which is fusion between between couples but it also may play an important role in companionship and group identity.

The Anti-Pheromone

Our concern for date rape and sexual assault has led to the consideration of the use of odor as a deterrent to sexual activity. While noxious or fecal odors can deter the most glorious pheromonal stimuli, it is not always adequate or readily available. What is necessary is the search for scents, preferably not grossly obnoxious, but if pheromones work via volatiles, "Anti-Pheromones" that could shut down our sexually meditating neuronal centers or blocking our response to them. This requires the search fore physiologically designed odors that can shut out dominating pheromonal influences by acting on its neuronal pathways to and from the brain.

For woman concerned with their security, fending themselves against sexual marauders or for those of us interested in maintaining the sexual virtue of our pubertal children, or in an alternative approach to population control, "Anti-Pheromones" might become the best birth control device satisfactory for parental, social, and religious interests. The search should be generated for the biologic equivalent of vomeronasal stuffed nose that leaves us free for gastronomic pleasure.

A world without pheromones or its influence could be a sad place to live in. It could in effect resemble a prison. A life without sexual anticipation represents a form of premature aging.

Our Sex Drive

From what does our sex drive spring? It essentially begins with adolescence when our budding sexuality is stimulated by erotic fantasy. If this is followed by masturbation and orgasm then our erotic motivation is reinforced by pleasure. However, what triggers erotic fantasy at any age? As an adult, it can be stimulated by what we see, but the other element is pheromonal, and sex-related odors probably form the beginning of childhood fantasies. What we observe in those affected by pheromone-based products is not only the enhancement of fantasy, but behavior motivated "sex drive" or "animal exuberance." How we respond to this instinctual drive depends on developing confidence to test one's fantasy in the real world. This is the pursuit of love!

What can we anticipate from the developing skills of the perfumers with their new physiologic knowledge of our vomeronasal (VOS) sensitivities when perfumes will commercially enter the area of love's rivalries with love potions that really work? How will they affect us? These human pheromones can both enhance the bonds of romantic affinities or thrust us adrift in a sea of conflicting desire. We must be concerned that this is the time where the perfumer will become the purveyor of love potions that really work! Romance may be entering an era where it can be bottled, and to those of us that have read this book, or are active in neuroscience and behavioral research, this should be of concern, but should not be surprising.

For the religious who see love as primarily a reproductive event; in contrast, for those that see women as second class citizens who must be protected from their animalistic desires; or, for those men that seek to exploit women, the availability of human pheromones will present problems. It will challenge all of us, including those that see our civilization and us as superior or completely distinct from that of animals. With the commercial availability of pheromone-related products, the genie is out of the bottle, and whether we view ourselves as creationists or Darwinians, it will be our responsibility to be entertained, not controlled by this bewitching genie.

Pheromones Encourages Bonding

In relation to the influence of pheromones, it is not that their influence is only on the mechanics of our sexuality: eroticism, copulation, oral sex, or heterosexual versus homosexual choice. As we will see in the examples that follow, pheromones are also responsible for encouraging the bonding that occurs between parents and their children, and even between surrogate parents and abandoned young in the animal kingdom.

In a recent issue of *Natural History* magazine, (Vol. 5, 2001) Sarah Blaffer Hrdy, in discussion of the interest of "Mothers and Others" regarding a mother's own, and related and unrelated offspring, speaks to a phenomenon of "cooperativity," where animal species develop supportive interactions wherein non-mothers, including males, provide strong supporting interactions with juveniles. This occurs sometimes regardless of family genetic origins or even species origin. For example, what, on occasion, prompts a dog to adopt and begin nursing kittens? What prompts animals as diverse as elephants and monkeys to collectively support the growth and development of the unrelated newborn, independently of a direct genetic bond? While Hrdy speaks of this as "cooperative breeding" and focuses on the empathy releasing activity of the child, she does not speak to this as the end result of pheromonal input. However, our children look good, and even smell good to us, regardless of poor sphincter control, and independently of whether we contributed directly to their existence.

Hrdy speaks of the work of Storey (Jan. 8, 2000, *New Scientist*) who has shown that, with pregnancy, testosterone levels go down and prolactin levels go up, in male partners of pregnant women. This can only be explained by pheromones of pregnancy, produced by the woman, influencing the male to enable him to accommodate the newborn child. Sexual intercourse is not involved but the previous remembered act of reproduction, reinforced by pheromones probably influences the male who remains on intimate terms with his pregnant partner.

Health benefits

What can be said of the potential health benefits from the use of these and similar pheromone-related products? As discussed earlier, according to Dr. Winnifred Cutler, there is some evidence to suggest that the use of viable pheromone products has some benefits, beyond sexual attraction. This includes a positive influence on menstrual cycles, fertility, as well as sexual attraction. In an article published in the *Journal of Continuing Psychiatric Education*, Dr. Cutler says, "Recent discoveries of invisible, odorless, sex attractants, called pheromones, offer biologic ways to use cosmetics for improving the lives of men and women." Moreover, Dr. Cutler conducted two double-blind, placebo-controlled experiments that "found that human pheromones, but not placebo, produced significant increases over baseline in sexual behavior involving a partner." In another study, Dr. Cutler found that "positive results were also reported in one medical sample of post-hysterectomy women taking hormone replacement therapy (HRT) and who had been complaining of loss of sexual attractiveness. Ironically, the study was halted when its leader determined that 70% of the women using the pheromone product showed improvement. Despite this positive demonstration of the influence of pheromones, Dr. Cutler also believes that medical professionals should be cautious in their recommendations regarding their use.

"Practitioners should use skepticism and discrimination in recommending pheromone products to their sexual therapy patients. Any products claiming that they are an 'aphrodisiac' arouse our curiosity, but should be treated with skepticism because this is a drug claim that is regarded by the Food and Drug Administration as illegal and no such studies have been reported. Many commercial products claiming they contain pheromone ingredients may actually contain the previously discussed boar pheromone and for some, may act as a repellent."

Certainly, future research and development with pheromone-based products will yield many applications in many areas of health and medicine. From current research already done, there are a number of potential uses for pheromone-related formulas. For example, Cutler, Preti, and Garcia have developed a patent (USP 5,155,045, 1992) utilizing androgenic and estrogenic related hormones originally derived from the underarm secretions of active males. These priming pheromones can be used to restore cyclic regulatory hormonal activity to irregular menstruating women, and may restore menstrual function, fertility, and sexual desire in perimenopausal and menopausal women. Once this research matures, clearly their implications for widespread applications could benefit many people.

Future uses for pheromones – in the treatment of smell disorders?

While to date there has not been a direct correlation made, it is interesting to consider that in the not too distant future, a new generation of pheromone-related products might be used in the treatment of "smell disorders," including some mental illnesses as serious as schizophrenia. For example, sensitivity to odor has been studied in case reports dealing with the abnormal sensitivity of schizophrenics to odors in their environment. It's also interesting to note that the medical literature suggests that people with schizophrenia often exude a palpable odor that differentiates them from healthy individuals. This is not so surprising as physicians historically have used odor in the past to diagnose diseases such as liver failure, diabetic acidosis, typhoid fever, and a variety of rare metabolic diseases.

In 1960, Smith and Sines set out to determine the cause of what they thought was a characteristic odor found in schizophrenics. This was in the days before we had developed the sensitive technology of high-pressure liquid gas chromatography. Instead, they used the sensitive noses of rats to distinguish between the sweat samples of schizophrenics and healthy individuals. However, a panel of human testers was also able to distinguish between the presence of these odors in schizophrenics in contrast to healthy people.

In 1969, Smith and his colleagues identified the sweat-based odor of schizophrenia as trans-3-methyl-2-hexenoic acid. Unfortunately, the follow-up to these observations is sparse. Kirschner and Pfeiffer in 1973, draw parallelisms between this and other diseases associated with an abnormal fatty acid product. After this, the trail goes cold, as this area of research into the etiology of schizophrenia was apparently not supported by the powers that be in the field.

The disease of "split personality" called schizophrenia consists of the following: instability of personal relations; inability to form social bonds; social hypersensitivity; perceptual disturbances; acute turmoil and panic; delusion formation; and withdrawal. Included in this, although controversial, one might add, abnormal mother-child relationships, abnormal family history, and biochemical abnormalities. Could schizophrenia also relate to a distortion of pheromonal odors?

As discussed earlier, it was Weiner, who in 1966 postulated a relationship between "external chemical messengers" or pheromones and the syndrome of schizophrenia. The rhinencephalon or limbic area of the primitive brain was thought to be abnormal in schizophrenia and Wiener reported on work where removal of large portions of this area in monkeys produced a syndrome suggestive or schizophrenia.

In support of Wiener's hypothesis, Heath and Leach advanced the idea that parts of the olfactory lobe may function abnormally in schizophrenic behavior. This focus for schizophrenic behavior was based on abnormalities in the area of the brain to which we are olfactarily anatomically allied.

To explain schizophrenia, to understand its psychosis versus normal behavior, one of the characteristics of civilized behavior is "response inhibition." This is part of the act of repression that extends cortical (rational) control over instinctual behavior that is asocial.

To be human, we have to know when to stop, or it can result in serious injury if aggression, fear, or sexual importuning gets out of hand. This requires a level of sensitivity to the response of others. In psychosis, these sensitivities are lost, as they are also lost in race riots, looting, rape, and war, where primitive reactions governed by rage or fear predominate. We see this in animal behavior, where odor combined with visual stimulation triggers aggression, sexual display, or conquest.

What happens in schizophrenia is "that perceptual moods are heightened and the emotional response invoked is intense." Alternatively, the focus of response can be limited to one area of perception at the expense of another, leading to the failure of the patients to integrate themselves into a coherent relationship to the world around them. "Everything is in bits" when sensory input cannot be integrated due to a sensory overload from one source or another.

Again, Wiener noted that in schizophrenia, where olfactory hallucinations are common, schizophrenic patients possessed of olfactory hallucinations could become violent.

In another area, the supposed irrationality to scent could be based on the possibility of scent hypersensitivity. A patient is described who stated his father and brother exuded an odor when they have sexual intercourse, and judging himself, he said, "My body is fetid."

Weiner suggests that in schizophrenia, we are perhaps dealing with a real sensitivity rather than an imagined olfactory event. The overpowering awareness of body or environmental odors is not necessarily imagined, but may be the result of a sensory hypersensitivity that contributes to delusions or emotional reactivity.

Contrary to "madness" as a delusion, on occasion, the patient may be telling the literal truth as he or she sees it. Even mentally stable individuals could hardly avoid developing some type of delusion if they were subjected to a sensory input persistently in conflict with reality.

As Weiner points out, the "antithesis between reality and delusion is not as clear cut as it seems." In other words, when the schizophrenic patient tells us that the world around him is distorted, it may be due to overwhelming olfactory or other forms of sensory hypersensitivity.

If we look at our own behavior, when external stimulation becomes unbearable, as healthy individuals, we tend to withdraw. We cover our ears, or noses and eyes. Schizophrenics, then, can be so overwhelmed by olfactory and other stimuli that emotional indifference may also eventually supervene. In turn, the loss of odor sensitivity characterizes senile dementia and Parkinson's disease. Apart from loss of perception, does this include failure to generate pheromones?

Scent sensitivities

In support of the above, there are case histories of individuals whose olfactory sensitivity was extraordinary: For example, Freud's case of the "Rat Man" who, as a child, was able to recognize everybody by scent. The following are some examples, as described by patients, quoted from Wiener's extensive review.

"I often know whether a person has been in a room within the past hour or so by their odor."

"I can locate people by their perfume and my good husband has found it embarrassing when I tell him where he has been by the odor he has retained on his clothes or skin." How many "wayward" husbands have exposed their infidelity by just such wifely sensitivity to odor on their skin?

Weiner sites Kalmus, who reported on a blind girl working in a laundry who was able to recognize and identify the clothes she sorted by their odor. He cites this blind and deaf girl as being able to distinguish 50 of 57 different textile fabrics based on the odor of the dyes.

He describes individuals whose extraordinary sensitivity to odor makes them sick. In that sense, Wiener anticipated the origin of the school of Ecological or Environmental Medicine that associates illness with allergic sensitivity to minute levels of chemicals in our environment. Most physicians not trained to deal with these problems frequently feel this subset of patients who are environmentally hypersensitive, (i.e. to perfume, paint, or food odors), to be borderline psychotic.

Environmentally, many in medicine consider patients with this type of sensitivity disorder as "anxiety-ridden paranoiacs" and those doctors that service them and take them seriously, despite their credentials, are often called "quacks."

We agree with Weiner that schizophrenia may be due to the inappropriate entry of sensory stimulation into silent areas of the brain, sometimes called the "pre-conscious." In schizophrenia, normally silent areas of the brain involved in subconscious activity may be open to abnormal conscious awareness.

These observations are supported by more recent research that indicates that the auxiliary olfactory bulb attached to the vomeronasal receptor system is a repository of unconscious memory. Thus, pheromonal stimuli can affect behavior without our conscious awareness. If this were true, what would happen if the olfactory subconscious were to impinge too heavily on our conscious state? Would this result in disorder and confusion that would distort the conscious discipline of our minds, resulting in schizophrenia or apathy at one extreme? Alternatively it could induce a primitive olfactory aggression. Most strikingly, this happens to us when we are in love!

Along with the MOS, recent anatomic evidence for the above comes from a study that shows that schizophrenia involves the reduction in volume of the left temporal lobe of the brain. This was associated with loss of brain substance in the left anterior hippocampus, amygdala, and areas involved in odor perception (Shelton, et al, 1992).

Pheromonal input as it applies to love, or love-making, can be looked at as a form of madness! To summarize, odor and the power of scent is not incidental to the quality of our lives, but an integral part of what gives life quality. The loss or distortion of this sense may play a role in the pathophysiology of mental illness.

We believe there is an open horizon for continuing and future research in many areas where pheromones might be able to improve the health and well-being of many individuals. For instance, as Dr. Cutler mentions, the addition of using pheromones in conjunction with hormone replacement therapy (HRT) may provide menopausal women with the benefit of enhanced self-esteem or a renewed sense of well-being that could provide for the return or enhancement of sexuality. Knowing what we do about the intimate nature of bonding between parent and child, there may be a time where pheromone-derived perfumes may be used in relation to children who appear less responsive to their caregivers or vice versa. And, people who are partnered in intimate relationships may also benefit from the use of pheromone-related products, if there is a need to "jumpstart" the mutual attraction that brought them together.

Could nature adapt us to better handle sexual frustration by getting us to respond to olfactory stimuli? Perhaps pheromones in some cases, can be neutralizing or calming in their effects? Can a salivary, sweat or sebaceous activity signal our mental state to those around us? Would the use of pheromones be of value in subduing riotous crowds? Does this analogy also relate to human sexual frustration that leads to aggression, which in its minimal mode is associated with nagging and petulance, but at its extreme is violent.

As discussed, pheromones may be a component of schizophrenic delusion. With additional research and development, the possibility for the applications for pheromone-derived products is enormous.

Consider that while pheromone products can be used to attract others to us, different formulas could be designed to repel potential attackers. For instance, it might be possible to dispel rapists or turn off masculine aggressive sexuality as in "date rape" by releasing an odor, apart from fecal odors, which turns off sexual excitement. These odors would have to neutralize rage as well.

One inventor has developed a necklace containing a pod, that when broken releases a noxious odor that adheres to the woman to both repel and mark the sexual aggressor. With appropriate clinical research, the right odor may be found to be less injurious than mace, but possibly more effective as a deterrent.

Can couples use pheromones to enhance their sexuality; ration it? Can they use it to enhance their internal security and make loving optimal for either sex? Whether available pheromones will contribute to your "animal exuberance," "sex drive" or "libido," or "erotic fantasy," it is our view that its action will remain synergistic with our cortically brain-derived values. We will still need the erotic excitement of vision to provide its input, but at one level, that of kissing, nuzzling, and oral sex, pheromones will strongly influence our sexual behavior beyond its procreative role. We should remember that when we get close, as in kissing or oral sex, vision blurs, and yet, sex acts are equally thrilling for a blind man!

In regard to "cooperativity," promoting love of children and strengthening family values, I believe pheromone-related products will have a definite place. Again, as for its role, in the treatment of schizophrenia, and in the control of mob action, much has to be studied.

The possibilities and problems are clearly vast, but may be limited only by our imagination and creativity in finding ways to include pheromones as another means to increase our sense of well-being, our sexuality, and to improve all our relationships, as well as a means to someday help treat much more serious health issues.

Conclusion

> *"Sex contains all, bodies, souls, meanings, proofs, purities,*
> *delicacies, results, promulgations, songs, commands, health,*
> *pride, the maternal mystery, the seminal milk, all hopes,*
> *benefactions, bestowals, all the passions, loves, beauties,*
> *delights of the earth, all the governments, judges, gods,*
> *follow'd persons of the earth,*
> *These are contain'd in sex as parts of itself and*
> *justifications of itself."*
> — Walt Whitman

While much has been published in scientific journals in recent years about animal behavior related to odor, we found a paucity of material in regard to odor governing human behavior. This is what led us to explore the wide range of pheromonal expression in novels, poetry, and other literary forms regarding love. When it comes to human sexuality and romance, our poets and writers seem to have been able to grasp truths that had not yet been recognized by scientists who specialize in this field.

Our individual experiences in the realm of love or sex have validity that often anticipates sophisticated statistical laboratory research. What has inhibited our self-realization that we humans respond to pheromones has been our embarrassment at seeming to behave like animals in heat.

We like to think of ourselves as special acts of God's creation, superior to other animals. Ironically, as a result of our Judeo-Christian religious beliefs, we may have lost the base from which our humanness developed, as we repressed our awareness of sexual odors.

Fundamentalist religious faiths have made sex for pleasure or oral sex as something perverse and anti-family. However, for our lives to be better balanced, and to control exploitive population growth, we need a reappraisal that can provide us with an understanding of this aspect of sexuality as related to our instinctual roots. We have to see what has been described in the past as perversion has to now be seen as an integral part of our love for one another and not disparate from our religious and social conditioning.

Humans are unique, and what makes us this way is our capacity to experience our particular pheromonal odor preferences as cosmic, transcendental, and all encompassing. When odors are in sexual harmony, we feel chosen by God to enjoy this experience, and we are in love.

Love can relate to the effect of odor that contributes to our commitment to that "other" that holds us in our thrall. This odor affinity is the result of the natural incense that God has given us. We are human because our odor preferences are particularized, proximate, and focused.

The burning of punk, the smell of incense, or the Old Testament savor of a meat offering on the altar, is nothing compared to the sexually-mediated odors that encourage us to reproduce. Without these odors, we may be less successful as a species. We would find ourselves regimented further into isolation from each other, suffering the quiet desperation of a premature post-climacteric or menopausal fate that is socially, rather than endocrinologically induced.

Our genital secretions are meaningful beyond their procreative role, as they provide us with self-identity and stimulate our attraction to those we love.

As humans, we have as part of our social evolution put constraints on sexual behavior so important to our familial and species survival. However, with the knowledge of our evolutionary history, we should modify our ancient prejudices against oral sex or menstruation as a ritualistic pollution. Menstruation is another example of our unique humanness: it is not a curse or a mysterious event. With knowledge of sexual physiology, menstrual blood, and ejaculation of semen is not a loss of vital juices, or a polluting dangerous influence, but a hormonal event that signals sexual capacity via pheromonal output.

We must be aware that if we lose our sensitivity to sexual odors, or don't take advantage of them, we lose a salient feature of our capacity to love. As we grow older, we must recognize that the menopausal and climacteric changes associated with sex hormonal decline decrease our capacity to produce sebaceous or sexual secretions that mediate pheromone production. To be aware of this is to be able to change our circumstances, with hormone supplementation, pheromonal-boosted perfumes or just enthusiastic attention to what God has given us.

It is exciting to postulate that proximate pheromonal production with its hidden estrus allowed human females to select mates for their intelligence or child rearing participation rather than brawn. Reciprocally, human males were freed from the aggressive competitive stimulus induced by more potent female pheromones. This change in pheromone sexual signaling to the proximate, the need for closeness, slowed down the focused aggression between males competing for the opportunity to obtain a frenetic transient copulation.

Our enjoyment of perfume, the smell of flowers, the odors of the verdant world, must now encompass those pheromonal attractants that truly govern our relationship to each other. Flowers use their color, their shape, and their scent, to attract insects, birds, and bats to effect fertilization via pollenization. As humans, evolution has provided a similar pathway, that brings us together with fertilization (reproduction), as its goal.

Historical considerations:

We are all aware that science moves forward on the basis of previous findings. However, in the case of human sexuality it is only within this past century that our release from prudery and our growing understanding of hormonal and neuroendocrine effects on behavior and sexual morphology have enabled us to study our own behavior in a rational manner.

Although sex is one of the most important topics related to our survival and personal happiness, it has taken centuries for us to even to begin understanding the mechanisms by which human sexuality makes its presence manifest.

Lacoeur, in his history of human sexuality, points out that until the 18th century men and women were thought to be essentially the same. The difference between the sexes was only that women had internalized their male-like genitalia. However, during that century, it became well established that our genitals were distinctly anatomically different by gender.

Up until the 16th century, pregnancy was thought to require male "heat" for conception to occur. It then became apparent that pregnancy could occur without female orgasm; it was thought that the male's semen or "heat" ejaculated with vigor was what fired up the feminine element residing in the oven of the womb, which resulted in pregnancy.

Following the discovery of the microscope in the 17th century, sperm was observed to be carrying the "homunculus," the minuscule complete human form that took root in the incubator womb. In the 19th century the discovery of the human ovum gave women an equal share in fertilization. However, it was in the 19th century that women were now medically declared "the weaker sex" which denied many of them to this day their equal share in the pleasures of sexuality. This nonsense has persisted even into our own time, but is fortunately changing.

Another myth entrenched in 19th century medical thinking, which today fortunately is laughed at, was the detrimental effect of masturbation. The concept was based on the idea that sperm was a limited masculine resource, finite in quantity that had to be banked. If you exhausted your semen collateral, you suffered eventual debilitation. Unfortunately, this is still a concept that worries millions of men in the Indian subcontinent and we mention this only to provide an additional perspective of how slowly our understanding of human sexuality has developed.

Another example of how little, until recently, we understood our own sexual physiology is the fact that we knew nothing of the controlling elements governing the monthly sequence of ovulation until the 1930s. Until this was understood, the "safe" period to avoid conception was thought to be in the middle of the monthly cycle, and the period associated with menses was thought to be the fertile one.

It is only now that we understand menstruation as a programmed death of cells lining the uterus, when hormonal levels fall below a sustaining threshold. However, until a year or two ago, menstruation was thought to be due only to contraction of the uterine blood supply. We now understand programmed cell death where hormones control apoptosis (a signal for cell destruction). Similarly, we have just learned that our penile erections are produced by a gas, nitric oxide, released via neural stimulation of the vascular lining of the penile blood supply.

The Kinsey Report came out in 1948, and it is only since the 1960s that birth control pills, based on the correct knowledge of sexual cycling, have come into common usage, thus creating our contemporary sexual revolution. Concomitant with the sexual revolution has been the diminution of censorship under the broader interpretation of the First Amendment.

With the availability of explicit literature and films, we have had a growing reversal of negative feelings regarding alternate sexual behavior, such as that involving oral sex.

Our knowledge of the physiology of sex is burgeoning so that it was only at a symposium in 1991 that the myth of the vestigial nature of the vomeronasal organ was largely put to rest. Although still questioned by some, we feel we have a pheromonal detection system in our noses similar to that in any mammal. Humans may have vomeronasal sensitivity on par to that of cats and dogs, making oral sex, fellatio and cunnilingus a part of our loving sexual performance.

The past few years have called our attention to the terminal nerve, another sensory scent detection system that physiologically governs the sexual behavior of sharks, fish, amphibians, and reptiles. Its role in mammals deserves greater attention. The terminal nerve contains luteinizing hormone-releasing hormone (LHRH), a neuropeptide involved in sexual cycling governing ovulation and prostatic hypertrophy. It may be that functions of the terminal nerve have been encompassed in our vomeronasal (VNO) system.

We are now beginning to understand the multiple roles of hormonal agents, peptides or steroids. Many of our hormones have dual roles, depending on the physiologic state or age of the animal. Neuropeptides or neurotransmitters, once thought to be involved only in circadian (daily) or seasonal rhythms of sexual cycling, are now found to alter blood flow and aging.

The brain, long known to be influenced by steroid hormones, is now known to synthesize them. Lymphocytes, involved in host resistance to infection and immunity, are now seen to be producing opiate-like endorphins and trophic hormones thought at one time to be the exclusive province of the brain.

What was once anatomically separated is now a physiologic whole. Mind and body are one; nerve cells, endocrine glands, and white blood cells speak to one another. Based on this, it is not surprising that we can present a case for olfaction as a key sensory controlling factor governing our sexual destiny. Our nose is attached to the olfactory bulb and its accessory systems that lead directly to the brain; the nose is a conduit that influences our individual psyches.

Olfaction provides a direct connection to our behavioral agenda in connection to the outside world. In evolutionary development, chemically mediated responses related to smell, were the first to govern one-celled and early multi-cellular organisms. As humans, in evolution, we don't always abandon early systems vital to survival but co-opt and reutilize them.

The thrust of this book has been to make us realize that sexual odors or pheromones are a key factor to our sexual behavior. Obviously, we feel that recognition of this will serve, not only in a way that will initiate new frontiers of psychotherapy, but this knowledge will be equally important to one's own interpersonal behavior. Again, we feel that this helps to explain kissing and oral sex that have appeared to so many of us as bizarre and perverse behavior.

An understanding of pheromonal action can help us attain empathy for those with a sexual orientation different from our own. It should re-enforce the necessity of providing women with equal political and social rights and teach us more about male aggression and the constructive elements that govern our attraction for each other.

While our sex therapists and their manuals propagate new freedoms, they do not adequately explain why we humans behave as we do. We are, to an extent, still stuck with Freudian explanations from the earliest part of this century, wherein reproduction was the alpha and omega of human sexuality and oral sex and masturbation were considered perversions, and while homosexuality was barely tolerated or discussed. An understanding of pheromonal action can hopefully separate us from antiquated theories based solely on Oedipal mythology and penis envy.

What initially prompted our interest in the role of odor in human sexuality were personal, but isolated observations. These incidents stimulated us to think about the manner in which human sexuality was related to odor. Moreover, these experiences led us to wonder if others have made similar observations.

To recapitulate: a male bisexual friend returned to a homosexual orientation after an apparently successful three-year marriage. This man, although in an apparently loving heterosexual relationship with his wife, abruptly abandoned her for an open homosexual lifestyle. When queried, he said that he lost interest in his wife because he didn't like "the way she smelled." In contrast, the odors of his homosexual friends were appealing.

Recalling fifty years later, the odor of a seven-year-old girlfriend. As a child, I was enamored with the glorious smell emanating from her sweaty neck. I resorted to tickling this innocent focus of my excitement. This Proustian memory, related to skin and sweat, but not genitals, emphasizes the possibility that subtle odors can determine early preferences with an effect on gender response even before sexual maturity.

The sudden remembrances some 50 years later, that the odors we smelled in our parents bed, as we joined them as three-year-old children on Sunday mornings, were sexual and generated by their lovemaking.

The observation that a two-year-old's blanket collected body odors that were masturbatory in origin. The blanket nap was pushed by the child into her nostrils and given to her parents to share this genital smell as a social gesture. Again, we frequently observe the major chagrin of our two-year-olds when their blankets or teddy bears are washed, thus destroying their comforting smells.

Related to the above, the embracing and holding of an article of clothing impregnated with the scent of our lover can at times substitute for that person. As noted, Goethe during his *strum und drang* period, told his inamorata, who was going on a journey, to not wash her bodice, but to loan it to him. At 21, she married him.

The observation as adults that sexual odors remain on fingers, moustache, or beard, to provide a long-term pleasant reminder of genital secretions produced by passionate touching and embracing hours before.

Knowing that our lover has entered a crowded room by her scent. Does such an experience govern "love at first sight?" We believe that it is frequently not just sight alone, but also smell.

Many of us have memories of our squirming away or struggling as children to avoid body contact with members of the same sex, or that of an overly affectionate aunt or uncle. Could it be that we were trying to escape body odor, sexually defined, as a non-smoker tries to avoid cigarette smoke?

The declaration by a widowed friend, "I was popular as a young girl and dated many men, but I fell in love with Ed because I liked the way he smelled."

Consider the reactivity of a cat to catnip wherein odor alone produces a "drunken" state, somewhat equivalent to sexual ecstasy. In addition, the not infrequent embarrassing behavior of male dogs to human sexual odors.

The statement of a woman physician: "If I don't like the smell of a man, if he imposes it on me, it is an invasion of my privacy, like cigarette smoke in a 'no smoking zone.' More deadly, it is the rape of my intimate boundaries." Consider the transgression of a presidential lover who saved her semen-stained dress that almost led to an act of impeachment. Why did she save that dress? Our guess is that it was her desire to relive the experience through the odor.

The above observations, which many of us share, have stimulated our interest and fascination with human sexual odors as a factor in our lives. This was re-enforced by studies we did involving the unrelated physiology of hearing. We found that humans possess the capacity to perceive ultrasonic frequencies, above the acoustic range of the inner ear. With appropriate experiments our work showed that we have the residual capacity to hear independently of air conduction, as reptiles do, at frequencies high above the limits of mammalian air conducted (inner ear) perception. Hearing is conducted through bones and skin!

We now know that the navigation of creatures as diverse as bees, sharks, fish, salamanders, and birds can be governed by electrical or magnetic fields, at thresholds of sensitivity so weak as to be almost unimaginable. Birds, previously thought to be incapable of odor responses, are now found to use odor as a navigational map, and vultures may find their food by odor release.

It is obvious that, if we can hear like reptiles through skin and bone, and birds can smell, if evolutionarily speaking, our reptilian heritage for perceived sound is still functional, then why isn't it possible for odor sensibilities observed in lower animals to be operational in humans?

This thought, which up until 1991 had been speculative, is now anatomically and physiologically sound. The erroneous dogma, although still controversial, that the vomeronasal organ (VNO), the receptor for sexual odors in animals, was only vestigial in humans is no longer absolute. This specialized pheromonal receptor is now found in to be present in almost all men and women. It is found in the anterior one-third of our nasal septum, and its accessibility now provides us with electrophysiological methods for systematically identifying human pheromones.

It is our hypothesis that we are largely defined as men or women because of the way we smell and perceive our sexual odors. What has been missing has been our capacity to study and explore this olfactory heritage identified in all species, and surviving in our own behavior. Of interest, pheromones do not necessarily produce a subjective odor awareness, but stimulate our subconscious without rational memory.

For historical accuracy, we once more refer our readers to the provocative 1966 papers of Harry Weiner, who coined the term "olfactory sub-conscious," who speaks of the nonverbal language of scent generated by our bodies as a possible factor in the origin of schizophrenia.

Certainly, the role of pheromones in animal territoriality and hormonally induced aggression may explain the madness of crowds as related to a vomeronasal event involving human pheromones produced by the collective response of crowds at mass events.

We ought to be aware that our sexual agenda, governed by pheromones effects our time sense, where minutes seem like hours, or hours appear to be minutes, resulting in a world where time can be controlled by the presence of the one we love. Sexual attracting and longing involves not only a visible aesthetic, but a nasal one as well.

The inability to produce sexual odors, or our loss of interest in them, may be more a factor in divorce than money problems, mother-in-laws, or bad habits. Impatience and restlessness that cause us to seek new partners may reside in our failure to respond to the arousal and relaxation induced by home grown pheromonal influences.

For most of us, the fear of the hereafter, punitive laws, finances, and a parental or social conditioning helps to ensure the family bond. True, our social and religious structures hold us together beyond the more immediate attraction produced by sexual odors, but we should not fail to be aware of the social importance of odor bonding so long ignored by our religious leaders.

Religious injunction that separates the sexes, during prayer permits reflection. You cannot concentrate on God, the hereafter, and the threat of the devil and damnation in the temple, if pheromones are titillating your olfactory receptors, or when seductive perfume is wafting between the pews. It is obvious that religions that mix the sexes during prayer may be more social than contemplative.

The interest in anal sex ceases to be a perversion, but an odor preference related to anal secretions that override fecal odors or are obscured by them when hedonic loss of rationality related to pleasure preoccupies us with the erotic quality of penis, buttocks, or vagina. The pelvis is not a cesspool, but a blend wherein pheromonal attraction can prevail over excretory negativity.

Our genitals are not just visual releasers of sexual behavior, but they are wicks, disseminating odors that arouse us and divorce us from rationality or time constraints. Genital and facial hair are designed to release or entrap sexual odors.

This book is not written to minimize Freud's contribution, although it bemoans his having missed odor as a factor in his psychoanalytic thinking. Despite his close friendship with Fleiss, both missed the true significance of nasal structures as sexually responsive receptors to pheromones.

In rethinking odor as a factor in human sexual development, we now open our therapeutic interest in how this knowledge can be used to help people. "Smell" and "scent" is integral to our social and sexual heritage! It patently influences our social, as well as our asocial behavior.

In certain ways, odor provides a new place for Jungian collective consciousness. Unfortunately, what limits our awareness of odor's place in our folklore and legends is the limitation of our ability to express the quality of sexual odor and its awareness in our vocabulary.

How does one describe the nuance of odor? We need a more adequate vocabulary. But even without the words, pheromonal performance and memory do not necessarily reach our consciousness, although we are pre-programmed to respond to their stimulation in a subconscious manner.

Humans are, indeed, different from animals because we repress much of our sexual behavior. In the right erotic setting, we behave like animals, but in the social interplay of our daily lives, we function as if these odors have no effect upon us. This is the true repression that Freud missed in his theoretical constructs that made the subconscious the focus of psychoanalytic theory, and gave us insight to so much of human behavior.

Freud's penile envy, as a factor in female identity, should be replaced by the subtle influences of sweat, fatty acids, or steroid sebaceous secretions that separate male from female in a qualitative way, and direct our attention to heterosexual or homosexual attachment.

The trophic influences of the mother's body odors, seen in the light of rodent behavior, may be more important than Oedipal or more specifically, anal or genital fixation as factors in childhood social development.

The loss of male interest in aging women, or a woman's loss of sexual interest with age, may be less an effect of the loss of youthful figure and more a decline in pheromonal or copulin quality or odor awareness as motivating factors in sexual performance or romantic love. Certainly, it should continue to motivate the perfume industry to come closer in the scents they provide to the biologic reality existent in enjoying our own natural products.

Sexual identity, preference, and performance develop in response to odor clues as defined by volatiles or chemicals generated by our bodies. These odors are produced by skin or specialized glands, under the influence of sexually-identifying hormones. They are the products of sebaceous (oil glands) sweat, saliva, skin, expired air from our lungs, anal, urine and sexual secretions or excretion.

The bacteria and microflora that share our existence and contribute to the breakdown of the skin itself and secreted products from our skin, mouth, hair, vagina, and penis influence these odors.

If sexually-produced odors, governed by hormone production can alter the socializing of mice, rats, and other animals, if it can produce responses as diverse as aggression and territoriality, and yet govern maternal bonding and family identity in rodents, sheep and other mammals, why can't it influence us as well?

Anatomically, this now makes sense, as we are now aware that we humans possess a sensory system that is aesthetically responsive to the odors produced by our bodies. The importance of odor in sexual response is seen in the dual action of the neuropeptide LHRH (Leutinizing Hormone Releasing Hormone). This key hormone modulates odor and stimulates ovulation and related sexual responses in animals. This hormone, which is found throughout the olfactory system, also effects blood flow and blood pressure influencing the mammalian brain and body, and we must examine its interrelated effects on our sexual responses.

Most importantly, instead of seeing homosexual or bisexual preference as an environmental developmental problem caused by overprotective mothers, punitive fathers, or some subtle malfunction in social influences, it becomes simple if we see this as an odor preference, governed by olfactory maps in the brain that have not been kept in balance with genital anatomic identity.

Will our new awareness of odor as a gender identifying and sexually-modulating influence effect psychoanalytic theory and our lives? We certainly hope it will provide a new level of sympathetic understanding for homosexual, transvestite, and transsexual behavior and for those whose sexual focus centers on the anus, feet, leather, or rubber. We feel that this behavior of our sexual minorities relates to a disparity between their odor map, anatomic identity, and odor sensitivity and preference.

At the very least, an awareness of pheromones in our lives makes kissing and oral-genital sexual activity, while instinctive, a rationally understood event central to our being human.

It is our conviction that we have explained the origin of homosexuality as an in utero or neonatal event governing gender identity. This is an instinctive pattern, related to a "love map" no different from that of any other animal. Although this will create major controversy; if our sexual behavior is the result of pheromone influence stimulating same sex responses, this might be pharmacologically modifiable. However, one must ask if there is a voluntary desire or demand for a pharmacologically induced change that is not based on religious stricture?

There are drugs in hand that have shown modification of sexual choice and performance in animals, and they are readily available for testing in humans.

The expression of our sexual identity as a behavioral event can be disparate from morphologic identity. The absence or a decrease in the timed influence of male hormones on embryonic development seems to be a central event in male homosexuality which can be influenced by maternal stress and/or other endogenous factors. What is important is that early childhood and adolescent experience are less important than predispositions that are programmed to affect us in the womb. From the time of our conception, our sexual identity, influenced by the male hormone, causes us to spring forth at birth, with a well-defined sexual agenda. It takes sexual maturity for the sexual agenda to fully reveal itself, although there is evidence for pre-pubertal predisposition that explains gender identity governing heterosexual or homosexual behavior.

Will sexually defined odors apart from gender preference provide new clues as to aggression and passivity? Will it give us new insights into the cause of sexual abuse, rape, persecution of minorities and the madness of crowds? What about love and its irrationality?

Our sexual identity and performance needs the stimulation of sexual awareness and eroticism that are largely visual or auditory. In that regard, we are not that disparate from our primate relatives; men respond to "vaginal pink," breasts, areola, lips, eye gaze, waist, hips, and buttocks. Women certainly respond to variations of the above and to the appearance of male genitals or muscle. The timbre of one's voice is also involved in the above.

What has been missing from our understanding of the erotic has been the place of sexual odors, pheromones, some of them beyond our conscious recall, tickling our sexual subconscious. Some pheromones are apparent to us, acrid or subtle, pleasant or unpleasant, but available to our consciousness if looked for or indulged in with oral sex as the clue.

It is this power of scent that identifies our sexual preference and brings us together in love, romance and familial bonding, but, unfortunately, it can also destroy us by stimulating aggressive rage.

Our effort in putting this book together has given us the opportunity to see our closeness to our primate relatives. We have speculated that Darwinian female sexual selection focused on the size of male genitals, thereby paradoxically influencing the size of our brains. In similar fashion, the loss of violent competition for females, with the evolutionary decline of a visible human female estrus, so evident in chimpanzees, has enabled men to cohabit in a way that permits social stability and bonding which helped create civilization and the family unit. Now that current youthful (adolescent) ardor has resulted in oral sex, frequently becoming a substitute for penetration, it is appropriate that it be seen not as a quick, frequently immature substitute for relationships but as a fundamental process essentially leading to bonding and love.

Oral sex and orgasm catalyzed by pheromonal or copulin production is unique to humans as a prime motivating event in holding us to each other and deserves serious study as to its affect on the stability of human relationships and the role of pleasure in our lives as distinct from intromission as a reproductive event.

We must of course, be aware of the dangers involved if our chemists or perfumers succeed in rivaling our body's production of our own pheromones or copulins. If synthesized and made generally available, these chemically synthesized pheromones could be like giving vodka to an alcoholic, or heroin to an addicted public. Alternatively, therapeutic uses could be found, as we learn to identify and determine the different actions of pheromonal-based products.

We now benignly see perfumes as adjuncts to adornment and fashion, or a coverup for excretoary odors. They are more than that: perfume preferences with pheromones or copulins at their core can provide a tool to manipulate our behavior. The danger of their unrestricted or unwise use is that pheromones available as commercial odors could orchestrate our limbic control, producing an unrestrained regression to basic animal behavior.

We must remember the voyage of Odysseus and the spell of Circe, who turned Odysseus' men into animals. What saved Odysseus from enslavement as an animal, was a flower whose scent he inhaled which protected him from Circe's spell. This flower represents in legend what is true for pheromones' place in the reality of our human existence.

We are the products of our odors, and they are distinctly identifying in men, women, and children. These odors released by hormonal signals, or by pleasurable touch or emotional feeling are keys to our fundamental reproductive and social strategies. It is our awareness of human pheromonal odors and our ability to suppress or stimulate our responses to them that make us uniquely creative and, in evolutionary terms, distinct but related to our animal neighbors.

Afterword

If it were not for our interest in passion, this book would never have been written. Is passion a function of the irrational, the subconscious that makes a wish list of virtue in our mates charm, beauty, education, and income truly irrelevant to what really brings us together? In our sexual choices, are we compelled to select certain partners because of odor preference?

Why do we kiss, nuzzle, and move our way down, to engage in oral sex? Do we do these things as a response to the irresistible smell that our lover gives off from their skin and hair? Why does sexual odor cling to our undergarments, our hair, beard, and skin? What motivates homosexual love instead of a heterosexual one? Are we born with "love maps" that provide brain patterns that governs our choice of future mates? Are these choices influenced by sexually stimulated odors? Do these scent patterns that we are born with, at maturity, act synergistically with our vision or voice to stimulate our pairing, child rearing, and reproductive life?

We believe that all of the above dynamics can be explained by pheromones. All of us produce odors that draw us to one another stereotypically as a moth to a flame. The compelling attraction we feel for our lovers is not much different from what our dogs and cats do when they are in "heat."

Why has it taken us so long to recognize the power of sexually stimulated smells? For many of us, this recognition may be embarrassing, yet it is these sexual odors that play an important role in the universal dance between lover and the beloved. These smells and their influence reflect who you are, male or female, straight or gay.

Pheromones provide a pathway to passion and orgasm wherein the aesthetic of moisture, smell, and touch removes us from the mundane world. With vomeronasal receptors in our nose as a portal, pheromones divorce us from the rational and time stands still, as we leave this world to enter another. In this impassioned state, our limbic, non-thinking brain prevails!

We must recognize that at times we are given the choice to choose between instinct and logic. Pheromones provide us with a primordial escape that does not involve the hazards of drugs or alcohol. Equally narcotic, pheromones are nature's way of providing a sensuous gateway to a transcendent state that paradoxically gives us great pleasure and also encourages us to pair off and allows our civilization to develop and the human race to survive. Paradoxically, although reproduction is central, an odor aesthetic is also critical to human survival and familial bonding.

Pheromones are a key element in bonding that makes love extend itself beyond sexuality to concern itself with children, family, and friends. Now becoming available commercially as human pheromone-based perfumes, perhaps pheromones can provide us with a new way to view or renew our closest relationships. As complex as the nature of intimate bonding is in these close relationships, pheromone-based perfumes will no doubt present an additional challenge. Much like the genie in the bottle, once released, it will be up to each of us how to learn to use the magic and promise it holds for us.

General Resources

Bibliography

Historic: Reviews

Bloch, I. Das sexuallaben unserer Zeit in seinen Beziehungen zur modernen Kultur. Berlin: 1908, L. Marcus, 1980.

Freud, S.: Bemerkungen uber ginen fall von Zwangsneurose, Ges. Schr 8: 350, 1908.

Krafft-Ebing, R.: Psychopathia Sexualis Basic Books, New York, 1937.

Brill, A.A.: The sense of smell in the neuroses and psychoses. Psychoanalytic Q 1: 7-42, 1932.

Kinsey, A.C.; Pomeroy, W.B. and Martin, C.E.: Sexual behavior in the human male. W.B. Saunders, Phila pp. 177-178, 1948.

Freud, S.: Three essays on the theory of sexuality. Standard Edition, V. 7, 1949[VP1].

P.H. Hoch and J. Zubin: Psychosexual development in health and disease. Grune and Stratton, New York, 1949.

Freud, S. Letters: The Origins of Psychoanalysis Letters to Wilhelm Fliess, Drafts and Notes: 1887-1902, Basic Books, Inc. New York, 1954.

Webster, R. Why Freud Was Wrong. Basic Books, New York, 1995.

Sexual and Social Behavior: The Role of Odor and Other Events

Walton, A.H.: Aphrodisiacs from legend to Prescription. Associated Booksellers, 1958.

Parkes, A.S.: Sex, Science and Society. Oriol Press, Newcastle on Tyne, 1966.

E.E. Maccoby: The Development of Sex Differences. Stanford Univ. Press, Stanford, CA, 1966.

Seeboek, T.A.: On Chemical Signs: to Honor Roman Jakobson Mouton, The Hague, Paris, 1967. pp 1775-1782.

Cheal, M.: Social olfaction: A review of the ontogeny of olfactory influences on vertebrate behavior. Behav. Biol. 15: 1-25, 1975.

Thornton, E.M.: The Freudian Fallacy Dial Press, New York, 1984.

Hogg, J.T.: Mating in Big Horn Sheep: multiple creative male strategies. Science 225: 526-529, 1984.

Masson, J.M.: The complete letters of Sigmund Freud to Wilhelm Fleiss 1887-1904, Belknap/Harvard, Cambridge pp 161-162, 1985.

Carter, C.S. and Getz, L.L.: Monogamy and Prarie Vole; Scientific American, June 1993 pp. 100-106.

Boss, D.: The Evolution of Desire. Basic Books, New York, 1994.

Genes and Behavior

Weiner, J. Time, Love, Memory. Vantage Press, NY 1998.

Pheromones

Baur, B.A.B.: Woman and Love II: Boni and Liveright, New York, pp. 208-216, 1927.

Daily, C..D. and White, R.S.: Psychic reactions to olfactory stimuli. Brit. J.Med. Psychol. 10: 70-897, 1930.

Brill, A.A.: The sense of smell in the neuroses and psychoses. The Psychoanalytic Q 1: 7-42, 1932.

Karlson, P. and Luschke, M.: Pheromones: A new term for a class of biologically active substances. Nature 183: 55-56, 1959.

Fitzherbert, J.: Scent and the sexual subject. Brit. J. Med. Pyschol. 32: 806-809, 1959.

Kalogerakis, M.G.: The role of olfaction in sexual development. Psychosomatic Med. 25: 420-432, 1963.

Parker, A.S.; Bruce, K.M.: Olfactory stimuli in mammalian reproduction. Science 134: 1049-1054, 1961.

Mykytowyycz, R.: Further observations on the territorial function and histology of the submandibular cutaneous (chin) glands in the rabbit. Anim. Behav. 13; 400-412, 1965.

Mainardi, D.; Marsan, M.; Pasquali, A.: Causation of sexual preferences of the house mouse. The behavior of mice reared by parents whose odour was artificially altered. Atti Soc. Ital Sci. Nat Mus. Civico. di Sturca Nat. Milano, 104: 325-338, 1965.

Michael, R.P.: The role of pheromones in the communication of primate behavior. Proc 2ⁿᵈ Congr Primat Atlanta, GA, 1968 V1 Karger, New York, 1968, pp 101-107.

Dixon, A.K. and Mackintosh, J.H.: Effects of female urine upon the social behavior of adult male mice. Anim. Behav. 19: 138-140, 1971.

Comfort, A.: Likelihood of human pheromones. Nature 230: 432-433, 1971.

Davies, V.J. and Bellamy, D.: The olfactory response of mice to urine and effects of gonadectomy. J. Endocr. 55: 11-20, 1972.

Carter, C.S.: Effects of olfactory experience on the behavior of the guinea pig. Anim Behav 20: 54-60, 1972.

Murphy, M.R.: Effects of female hamster vaginal discharge on the behavior of male hamsters. Behavioral Biology, 9: 367-375, 1973.

Birch, M.C. ed: Pheromones. North Holland, New York 1974.

Comfort, A.: The likelihood of human pheromones. In: Pheromones ed. M.C. Birch, North Holland, New York, pp. 386-396, 1974.

Brooksband, B.W.I., Brown, R. and Gustafsson, J.A.: The detection of 5a-androst-16-en-3a-OL in human male axillary sweat. Experentia 30: 864-865, 1974.

Michael R.P.; Bonsall, R.W. and Warner, P.: Human vaginal secretions, Volatile fatty acid content. Science 186: 1217-1219, 1974.

Leon, M.: Maternal Pheromones. Physiol. Behav. 13: 441-453, 1974.

Michael, R.P.; Bonsall, R.W. and Kutner, M.: Volatile fatty acids, "copulins" in human vaginal secretions. Psychoneuroendocrinology, 1: 153-163, 1975.

Doty, R.L.; Ford, M.; Preti, G.; and Huggins, G.: Human vaginal odors change in pleasantness and intensity during the menstrual cycle. Science 190: 1316-1318, 1975.

Neckers, L.M.; Zarrow, M.X., Myers, M.M. and Denenberg, V.H.: Influence of olfactory bulbectomy and the serotogenic system upon intermale aggression and maternal behavior in the mouse. Pharm. Biochem. Behav 3: 545-550, 1975.

Cheal, M.: Social olfaction: A review of the ontogeny of olfactory influences on vertebrate behavior. Behav. Biol. 15: 1-25, 1975.

Claus, R. and Alsing, W.: Occurrence of 5α-androst-16-en-3-one, a boar pheromone in man and its relationship to testosterone. J. Endocrin 68: 483-484, 1976.

Shorey, H.H.: Animal Communication by Pheromones. Academic Press, New York,1976.

Doty, R.L.: Mammalian Olfaction, Reproductive Processes and Behavior. Academic Press, New York, 1976.

Scalia, F. and Winans, S.S.: New perspectives on the morphology of the olfactory and vomeronasal pathways in mammals. In: Mammalian Olfaction, Reproductive Processes and Behavior (ed.) R.L. Doty. Academic Press, New York, 1976, pp 7-28.

Doty, R.L. (ed.) : Reproductive endocrine influences upon human nasal chemoreception: A review. In Mammalian Olfaction, Reproductive Processes and Behavior (ed.) R.L. Doty, Academic Press, New York, 1976, pp 295-321.

Schmidt, U.: Olfactory threshold and its dependence on the sexual status of the female laboratory mouse. Nature Wissen Schafften 65: 601, 1978.

Nyby, J.; Whitney, G.; Schmitz, S. and Dizinno, G.: Postpubertal experience establishes signal value of mammalian sex odor. Behavioral Biol. 22: 545-552, 1978.

Drickamer, L.C. and Murphy Jr., R.X.: Female mouse maturation: Effects of excreted and bladder urine from juvenile and adult males. Develop. Psychobiology 11: 63-72, 1978.

Dizinno, G.; Whitney, G. and Nyby, J.; Ultrasonic vocalization by male mice (mus musculus) to female sex pheromone: experimental determinants. Behavioral Biology 22: 104-113, 1978.

Keverne, E.B.: Olfactory cues in mammalian sexual behavior. In: Biological Determinants of Sexual Behavior. (ed.) J.E. Hutchinson, John Wiley, New York, 1978, pp. 727-783.

Kirk-Smith, M.; Booth, DA.; Carroll, D, and Davies, P.: Human social attitudes affected by androstenol. Res. Commun. Psychol., Psych. and Behavior 3: 379, 1978.

Michael, R.P. and Zumpe, D.: Biological factors in the organization and expression of sexual behavior. In: Sexual Deviation (ed.) F. Rosen, Oxford Univ. Press, New York, 1979, pp. 441-480.

Johnston, R.E. and Coplin, B.: Secretion and other substances in golden hamsters. Behav. and Neural Biol. 25: 473-489, 1979.

Drewett, R.F. and Spiter, N.J.: The sexual attractiveness of male rats. Olfactory and behavioral components. Psychology of Behavior. 23: 207-209, 1979.

Cattarelli, M. and Chanel, J.: Influence of some biologically meaningful odorants on the vigilance states of the rats. Physiol & Behav. 23: 831-838, 1979.

Wysocki, C.J.: Neurobehavioral evidence for the involvement of the vomeronasal system in mammalian reproduction. Neuroscience and Behavioral Reviews. 3: 301-341, 1979.

Dayne, A.P.: The attractiveness of harderian gland smears to sexually naïve and experienced male golden hamsters. Anim. Behav. 27: 897-904, 1979.

Goodwin, M.; Gooding, K.M.; and Regenier, F.: Sex pheromones in the dog. Science 203: 559-561, 1979.

Schleidt, M.: Personal odor and nonverbal communication. Etiology and Sociobiology. 1: 225-231, 1980.

Kirk-Smith et al. Effect of androstene on choice of location in others presence. H Van der Stabre (ed.) Olfaction and Taste. IRL Press, London, 1980.

Murphy, M.R.: Sexual preferences of male hamsters: Importance of preweaning and adult experience, vaginal secretion, and olfaction on vomeronasal sensation. Behavioral and Neural Biology 30: 323-340, 1980.

Norris, D.M. (ed.) Preception of Behavioral Chemicals. Elsevier/North Holland, New York, 1981.

Dunbar, I. and Carmichael, M.: The response of male dogs to urine from other males. Behav. And Neural. Biol. 31: 465-470, 1981.

Marshall, D.A., Blumer, L.; and Moulton, D.G: Odor detection curves for pentanoic acid in dogs and in humans. Clinical Senses 6: 445-451, 1981.

Doty, R.L.: Olfactory communication in humans. Chemical Senses 6: 351-376, 1981.

Schleidt, M.; Hold, B. and Attili, G.: A cross-cultural study on the attitude towards personal odors. J. Chem. Ecology. 7: 19-31, 1981.

Thody, A.J.; Donohoe, S.M.: and Schuster, S.: α-Melanocyte stimulating hormone and the release of sex attractant odors in the female rat. Peptides. 2: 125-129, 1981.

Pietras, R.J.: Sex pheromone production by preputial gland. The regulatory role of estrogen. Chemical Senses. 6: 391-408, 1981.

Engen, T.: The Perception of Odors. Academic Press Series in Cognition and Perception. New York, 1982.

Muller-Schwarze and D.; Silverstein, R.M.: Chemical signals: Vertebrates and aquatic invertebrates. Chemical Signals in Vertebrates. Plenum Press, 1979, 1982.

Cain, W.S.: Odor identification by males and females: Predictions vs Performance. Chemical Senses 2: 129-141, 1982.

Kirk-Smith, M.D., Van Toller, C. and Dodd, G.H.: Unconscious odour conditioning in human subjects. Biol. Psych. 17: 221-231, 1983.

Pedersen, P.E. Stewart, W.B.; Greer, C.A. and Shepherd, G.M.: Evidence for olfactory function in utero. Science 221: 448-480, 1983.

O'Connell, R.J. and Meredith, M.: Effects of volatile and nonvolatile chemical signals on male sex behaviors mediated by the main and accessory olfactory systems. Behavioral Neuroscience. 98: 1083-1093, 1984.

Clancy, A.N.: Coquelin, A.; Macrides, F.; Gorski, R.A. and Noble, E.P.: Sexual behavior and aggression in male mice. Involvement of the Vomernasal System. J. Neuroscience. 4: 2222-2229, 1984.

Young, S.: Are we led by the nose. New Scientist. Dec 1984, 32-37, 1984.

Filsinger, E.E.; Braun, J.J.; Monte, W.C. and Linder, D.E.: Human (homo sapiens) responses to the pig (Sus Scrofa) sex pheromone 5 Alpha-androst-16-en-3-one. J. Comp. Psych. 98: 219-222, 1984.

Hummel, H.E. and Miller, T.A. (ed.) <u>Techniques in Pheromone Research</u>. Springer Verlag. New York, 1984.

Albone, E.S and Shirley, S.C.: <u>Mammalian semiochemistry</u>: The investigation of chemical signals between mammals. Chichester (West Sussex), Wiley, New York, 1984.

Doty, R.L.: Gender and endocrine related influences upon olfactory sensitivity: In <u>Clinical Measurement of Taste and Smell</u> (ed.) H.L. Meselman, R.S. Rivlin MacMillan, New York, 1985.

Doty, R.: <u>The Primates III: Humans</u>. In: <u>Social Odours In Mammals</u>. (ed.) R.E. Brown, D.W. Mac Donald. Claredon Press, Oxford, 1985 pp 804-832.

Doty, R.L.; Applebaum, S., Zusho, H.; and Settle, R.G: Sex differences in odor identification ability. A cross-cultural analysis. Neuropsychologia 23: 667-672, 1985.

Epple, G.: The primates I: Order anthropoidea: social odours in mammals. Ed. R. E. Brown and D.W. MacDonald. 2: 739-769, Clarendon Press, Oxford, 1985.

Epple, G. and Smith III, A.B.: The Primates II: A case study of the saddle back tamar saguinus fusicollis. In: Social Odours in Mammals. (ed.) R.E. Brown, D.W. MacDonald 2: 770-803, Claredon Press, Oxford, 1985.

Corbin, A.: The Foul and the Fragrant: Odor and the French social of imagination. Harvard University Press, 1986.

Singer, A.G.: A chemistry of mammalian pheromones. J. Steroid Biochem Molec Biol. 39: 627-632, 1991.

Monti-Bloch, L.; Groser, B.I.: Effect of putative pheromones on the electrical activity of the human vomeronasal organ and olfactory epithelium. J. Steroid Biochem. Molec. Biol. 39: 573-582, 1991.

Sherpherd, G.M.; and Firestein, S.: Toward a pharmacology of odor receptors and the processing of odor images. J. Steroid Biochem. Molec. Biol. 39: 583-592, 1991.

Cowley, J.J. and Brooksbank, B.W.L.: Human exposure to putative pheromones and changes in aspects of social behavior. J. Steroid Biochem Molec. Biol. 39: 647-659, 1991.

Berliner, D.L.; Jennings-White, C. and Larker, R.M.: The human skin, fragrances and pheromones. J. Steroid Biochem. Molec. Biol. 39: 671-680, 1991.

Berliner, D. U.S. Patent 5,278,141, 1994.

Boehm, N.; Roos, J. and Gasser, V.: Luteinizing hormone releasing hormone (LHRH)-expressing cells in the nasal septum of human fetuses. Brain Res. Dev. Brain Res. 82: 175-180, 1994.

Wood, R.I. and Newman, S.W.: Integration of chemosensory and hormonal clues is essential for mating in the male Syrian hamster. J. Neurosci. 15: 7261-7269, 1995.

Smith, T.D., Siegel, M.I. and Burrows, A.M. et al. Searching for the vomeronasal organ of adult humans. Micro. Res. Tech. 41: 483-491, 1998.

Cutler, W.: Human sex-attractant pheromones: Discovery, Research, Development, and Application in Sex Therapy. Psychiatric Annals - The Journal of Continuing Psychiatric Education 29: 54-59, 1999.

Schwanzel-Fukuda, M.: Origin and migration of luteinizing hormone neurons in mammals. Microsc Res. Tech. 44: 2-10, 1999.

Keverne, E.B.: The vomeronasal organ. Science 286: 716-720, 1999.

Wysocki, C.J. and Preti, G.: Human body odors and their perception. Journal of Taste and Smell Research 7: 19-42, 2000.

Preti, G.: Human body odors and their perception. The Monel chemical Senses Center, Philadelphia. In press.

Kodis, M.; Love Scents, Dutton, New York, 2000.

Tissingh, G.; Berendse, H.W. and Bergmans, P. et al. Loss of olfaction in de novo and treated Parkinson's Disease: Possible implications for early diagnosis. Mov. Disord. 16: 41-61, 2001.

Turetsky, B.I.; Moberg, P.J.; Yousem, D.M. et al.: Reduced olfactory bulb volume in patients with schizophrenia. Am. J. Psychiatry 157: 828-830, 2000.

Chen, D., Havilland-Jones, J.: Human olfactory communication of emotion. Precept. Mot. Skills 91: 771-781, 2000.

Jacob, S. and McClintock, M.K.: Psychological state and mood effects of steroidal chemosignals in women and men. Horm. Behav. 37: 57-78, 2000.

Won, J., Mair, E.A., Bolger, W.E., Conran, R.M.: The vomeronasal organ: An objective analysis of its prevelance. Ear, Nose, Throat, 79: 600-605, 2000.

Trotier, D., Eliot, C.; and Wassef, M. et al.: The vomeronasal cavity in humans. Chem. Senses 25: 369-380, 2000.

Leinders-Zufall, T.; Lane, A.P.; and Puche, A.C. et al.: Ultrasensitive pheromone detection by mammalian vomeronasal neurons. Nature 405: 792-796, 2000.

Zbar, R.I.; Zbar, L.I.; Dudley, C.; et al.: A classification schema for the vomeronasal organ in humans. Plast. Reconstr. Surg. 105: 1284-1288, 2000.

Smith, T.D.; Bhatnagar, K.P.: The human vomeronasal organ Pt II Prenatal Development. J. Anat. 197: 3421-3436, 2000.

Bylinsky, G.: Technology to Watch: A Sixth Sense That Affects How You Feel. Moran, D.T. Pheromone Facts www.realfragrances.com, 2000.

Lyall Watson, Jacobson's Organ and the Remarkable Nature of Smell,, W.W. Norton & Company, 2000.

Rekwot, P.I.: Ogwu, D.; Oyedipe, E.O.; Sekoni, V.O.: The role of pheromones and biostimulation in animal reproduction. Anim. Reprod. Sci. 65: 157-170, 2001.

Knecht, T.M.; Kuhnau, D.; Huttenbrink, K.B.; et al.: Frequency and localization of the putative vomeronasal organ in humans in reaction to age and gender. Laryngoscope. 111: 448-452, 2001.

The vomeronasal system (VOS) and the vomeronasal organ (VNO).

Johnson, A., Josephson, R.; and Hawke, M.: Clinical and histological evidence for the presence of the vomeronasal (Jacobson's) Organ in adult humans. J. Otol. 14: 71-79, 1985.

Sanchez Criado, J.E. and Gallego, A.: Male induced precocious-puberty in the female rat. Role of Vomeronasal system. Acta Endocr. Suppl. 225: 255, 1979.

Wysocki, C.J. and Meredith, M.: In: T.E. Finger, W.L. Silver ed; The Vomeronasal System. Neurobiology of taste and smell. Chapt VI pp. 125-158, John Wiley, NY 1987.

Moran, D.T., Jafek, B.W. and Rowley, III., Carter, J.: The vomeronasal organ in man: Ultrastructure and frequency. Journal of Steroids, Biochemistry and Molecular Biology, 39: 552-545, 1991.

Stensaas, L.J.; Lavker, R.M.; Monti-Bloch, Grosser, B.I.; and Berliner, D.L.: Ultra structure of the human vomeronasal organ. J. Steroid Biochem. Molec. Biol. 39: 553-560, 1991.

Moran, D.T., Monti-Bloch, L.; Stensaas, L.J.; and Berliner, D.L.: Structure and function of the human vomeronasal organ In: R.L. Doty (ed.): Handbook of Olfaction and Gustation Marcel Dekker, NY pp. 793-820, 1995.

Smith, T.D.; Siegel, M.I.; Burrows, A.M. et al.: Searching for the vomeronasal organ of adult humans. Microsc. Res. Tech. 41: 483-491, 1998.

Smith, T.D. and Bhatnagar, K.P.: The human vomeronasal organ Pt II Prenatal Development. J. Anat. 197: 3421-3436, 2000.

Won, J.; Mair, E.A.; Bolger, W.E.; and Conran, R.M.: The vomeronasal organ: An objective analysis of its prevalence. Ear, Nose, Throat, J. 79: 600-651, 2000.

Trotier, D.; Eliot, C; Wassef, M.; et al.: The vomeronasal cavity in humans. Chem. Senses 25: 369-380, 2001.

Leinders, Zufall, T.; Lane, A.P.; Puche, A.C. et al.: Ultrasensitive pheromone detection by mammalian vomeronasal neurons. Nature. 405: 792-796, 2000.

Zbar, R.I.; Zbar, L.I.; Dudley, C. et al.: A classification schema for the vomeronasal organ in humans. Plast. Reconstr. Surg. 105: 1284-1288, 2000.

Lyall, W.: <u>Jacobson's Organ and the Remarkable Nature of Smell</u>. London: W.W. Norton & Co., New York, 2000.

Knecht, T.M.; Kuhnau, D.; Huttenbrink, K.B. et al.: Frequency and localization of the putative vomeronasal organ in humans in reaction to age and gender. Laryngoscope. 111: 448-452, 2001.

Nasreddin, D.; Abolmaali, D.K. and Knecht, M. et al.: Imaging of the human vomeronasal duct. Chem. Sens. 26: 35-39, 2001.

Sex Differences and Pheromones

Lloyd, B. and Archer, J.: Exploring Sex Differences. Academic Press, New York, 1971.

Bronson, F.H. and Marsden, H.M.: The preputial gland as an indicator of social dominance in male mice. Behav. Biol. 9: 625-628, 1973.

(Ed.) R.C. Friedman, R.M., Richard, R.L. Vandewiele, L.O. Stern: Sex Differences in Behavior. J. Wiley New York, 1974.

Jones, R.B. and Nowell, N.W.: A comparison of the aversive and female attractant properties of urine from dominant and subordinate male mice. Animal Learning and Behavior. 2: 141-144, 1974.

Hopson, J.L.: Scent signals: The silent language of sex. Wm. Morrow & Co., New York, 1975.

(Ed.) R.L. Doty. Mammalian Olfaction, Reproductive Processes and Behavior. Academic Press, New York, 1976.

Hoyenga, K.B. and Hoyenga, K.T.: The question of sex differences. Psychological, Cultural and Biological Issues. Little Brown & Co., Boston, 1976.

Shoren, H.H.: Animal communication and pheromones. Academic Press, New York, 1976.

Hutchinson, J.B. (ed). Biological determinants of sexual behavior. J. Wiley, New York, 1978.

Leibowitz, L.: Females, Males, Families. Duxbury Press N. Scituate Mass, 1978.

(Ed.) J.B. Hutchinson, Biological Determinants of Sexual Behavior. J. Wiley and Sons, New York, 1978.

Michael, R.P. and Zumfe, V.: Biological factors in the organization and expression of sexual behaviour. In: Sexual Deviation (ed.) I Rusen, Oxford Univ. Press, New York, 1979: pp 441-480.

Solheim, G.S.; Hensler, J.G. and Spear, N.C.: Age dependent contextual effects in short-term active avoidance retention in rats. Behavioral and Neural Biol. 30: 250-255, 1980.

Booth, W.D. and Baldwin, B.A.: Lack of effect on sexual behavior of the development of testicular function after removal of the olfactory bulbs in prepubertal boars. J. Reprod.
Fertil. 58: 173-182, 1980.

Pas, M.D.: A theory of erotic orientation and development. Psychological Rev. 88: 340-353, 1981.

Norris, D.M. (ed): Perception of behavioral chemicals. Elselvier/North Holland, New York, 1981.

Abramson, P.R., Perry, L.B.; Seely, T.T.; Seeley, B.M. and Rothblatt, A.B.: Thermographic measurement of sexual arousal: A discriminant validity analysis. Arch. Sexual Behavior. 10: 1717-176, 1981.

Engen, T.: The Perception of Odors. Academic Press, New York, 1982.

Muller-Schwarze (ed.) Chemical signals in vertebrates 3. Plenum Press, New York, 1982.

Russel, M.J.: Human olfactory communications pp. 259-273. In: Chemical Signals in Vertebrates (ed.) E. Muller-Schwarze, R.M. Silverstein, Plenum Press, New York, 1982.

Thornton, E.M.: The Freudian Fallacy. An alternative view of Freudian theory. Dial Press, New York, 1984.

Hummel, H.E. and Miller, T.A. (ed): Techniques in Pheromone Research. Springer-Verlag, New York, 1984.

(Ed.) K. Howells The Psychology of Sexual Diversity. Basic Blackwell, New York, 1984.

Cherfas, J.: How Important is the Family Smell: Report on Int. Ethological Conf., Toulouse, 1985. Work of Schaal, B. and Porter, R. New Scientist Oct 24, 1985, p 27.

Fillon, T.J. and Blass, E.M.: Responsiveness to estrous chemostimuli in male rats. J. Commu. Psychol. 99 328-335, 1985.

Brown, R.E. and MacDonald, D.W.: Social odours in mammals. Clarendon Press, Oxford, 1985.

Fillion, T.J. and Blass, E.M.: Infantile experience with suckling odors. Determines adult sexual behavior in male rats. Science 231: 729-731, 1986.

Novotny, M.; Jemiolo, B.; Harvey, S.; Wiesler, D. and Marchlewska-Koj, A.: Adrenal mediated endogenous metabolites inhibit puberty in female mice. Science 231: 722-725, 1986.

Money, J. Lovemaps, Irvington Publishers, Inc. New York, 1987.

Ackerman, D: A Natural History of the Senses. Vintage Books, 1990.

Stoddart B. The Scented Ape: The Biology and Culture of Human Odour. Cambridge Univ Press, 1990.

Calasso, R.: The Marriage of Cadmus and Harmony, Vintage International 1993.

Wright, R.: The Moral Animal: Pantheon, NY 1994.

Eberhard, W.: Female control: Sexual Selection by Cryptic Female Choice, Princeton, 1996.

Angier, N. Woman, An Intimate Geography, Houghton, Mifflin, Co. New York 1999.

Miller, G.: The Mating Mind, Doubleday, NY 2000.

Barash, P. and Lipton J.E.: The Myth of Monogamy. Fidelity and Infidelity in Animals and People. Freeman, New York, 2001.

Coolidge Effect

Wilson, J.R.; Kuehn, R.E and Berca, F.A.: Modification in the sexual behavior of male rats produced by changing the stimulus female. J. Comp. Physiol. Psychol. 561: 636-644, 1963.

Tiefer, L.: Copulatory Behavior of male Rattus Norvegius in Multiple Female Exhaustion Test   Anim. Behav. 17: 718-721, 1969.

Carr, W.J.; Hirsch, J.T. and Balazs, J.M.: Responses of male rats to odors from familiar versus novel females. Behav. & Neural Biol. 29: 331-337, 1980.

Child Development

Moll, A.: The sexual life of the child. (ed) E. Paul, pp.57-58, London, George Allen, 1912.

Lipsett, L.; Engen, T. and Kaye, H.: Developmental changes in the olfactory threshold of the neonate. Child Develpm 34: 371-376, 1963.

Bakwin, H.: Erotic feelings in infants and young children. Am. J.Dis.Child 126: 52-54, 1973.

Chael, M: Social olfaction: A review of the ontogeny of olfactory influences on vertebrate behavior. Behav. Biol. 15: 1-25, 1975.

Socarides JC - Massive Childhood Fears, Beyond Sexual Freedom, Quandrangle Books, New York 1975.

Reinisch, J.M.; Ziemba-Davis, M.; and Sanders, S.A.: Hormonal contributions to sexually dimorphic behavioral development in humans. Psychoneuroendocrinol 161: 213-278, 1994.

Homosexuality

Kinsey, A.: Sexual behavior in the human male. Saunders Phila, 1948.

Ford, C.S. and Berch, F.: Patterns of Sexual Beahvior. Harper & Bros., New York, 1951.

Hooker, E. The adjustment of the male overt homosexual. J. of Projective Techniques 21: 18-31,1957.

Bieber, I.I. et al. Homosexuality: A psychoanalytic Study of Male Homosexuals. Basic Books, New York, 1962.

Brautigam, W.: Kuperlich, Seelische and Soziale Einflusse Auf Die Geschlechtszuge-Horigkeit Des Menschn Der Internist 5: 171-182, 1964.

Ollendorff, R.H.V.: The Juvenile Homosexual Experience and Its Effect on Adult Sexuality. Julian Press, New York, 1968.

Bieber, I.: "Homosexuality" In (ed.) A. Freidman, H. Kaplan Comprehensive Textbook of Psychiatry, William and Wilkins, 1967, New York, pp. 973.

Hooker, E. "Homosexuality" Int. Encyclopdia of the Social Sciences. MacMillan Co., New York,1968.

Ovescy, L: Homosexuality and Pseudohomosexuality. Science House, New York,1969.

Socarides, C.: Psychoanalytic therapy of a male homosexual Psychoanalytic quartly 38: 173-1090, 1969.

Edwards, D.A.: Post neonatal androgenization and adult aggressive behavior in female mice. Physiol. Behav. 5: 465-467,1970.

Money, J.: Sexual dimorphism and homosexual gender identity. Psychol Bull. 74: 425-440, 1970.

Mascia, D.N.; Money,J. and Earhardt, A.A.: Fetal feminization and female gender identity in the testicular feminizing syndrome of androgen insensitivity. Arch. Sex Behav. 1: 131-142, 1971.

McDougall, J.: Primal scene and sexual perversion. Int. J. Psycho Anal 53: 371-384, 1972.

Money, J. and Ogunro, C.: Behavioral sexology: Ten cases of genetic male intersexuality with impaired prenatal and pubertal androgenization. Arch. Sex. Behav. 3: 181-205, 1974.

Friedman, R.C.; Richart, R.M.; and Vande Wiele, R.L. (ed.): Sex differences in behavior. J. Wiley, NY 1974.

Money, J. and Tucker, P.: Sexual signatures. Little, Brown & Co., Boston, 1975.

C.A. Tripp: The homosexual matrix. McGraw-Hill, 1975.

Money, J. and Schwartz, M.: Dating, romantic and nonromantic friendships and sexuality in 17 early treated adrenogenital females aged 16-26. In: Congenital Adrenal Hyperplasia. (ed.) P.A. Lee, L.P., Plotnick, A.A. Kowarski, C.J. Nigem, University Park Press, Baltimore pp. 419-431, 1977.

Ehrhardt, A: Behavior effects of estrogen in the human female. Pediatrics 62: 1166-1170, 1978.

Meyer-Bahlburg, H.F.L.: Behavioral effects of estrogen treatment in human males. Pediatrics 62: 1171-1177, 1978.

Freund, K.: A conceptual framework for the study of anomalous erotic preferences. J. Sex Marital Ther. 4: 3-10, 1978.

I. Rosen: Sexual deviation. Oxford Univ. Press, New York, 1979.

Meyer-Bahlurg, H.F.L.: Sex hormones and female homosexuality: A critical examination. 8: 101-119, 1979.

Imperato-McGingley, J.; Peterson, R.E.; Gautier, T. and Sturla, E.: Androgens and the evolution of male gender identity among male pseudohermaphrodites with 5α reductase deficiency. N.Eng. J. Med. 300: 1233-1237, 1979.

Stoller, R.F.: The Gender Disorders. Sexual Deviation. (ed.) I. Rosen, Oxford Univ. Press, New York, pp.109-138, 1979.

Baum, M.J.: Differentiation of coital behavior in mammals: A comparative analysis. Neuroscience and Biobehavioral Reviews. 3: 265-284, 1979.

Imperato-McGinley,J.; Peterson, R.E.; Leshin, M.; Griffin, J.E.; Cooper, G.; Draghi, S.; Berenyi, M. and Wilson, J.D.: Steroid 5α reductase deficiency in a 65 year old male pseudohermaphrodite. The natural history, ultrastructure of the testes and evidence for inherited enzyme heterogenecity. J. Clin. Endocrinol. Metab. 50: 15-22, 1980.

Storms, M.D.: Theories of sexual orientation. J. Personality and Social Psychol. 38: 783-792, 1980.

Bayer, R.: Homosexuality and American Psychiatry. The Politics of Diagnosis. Basic Books, New York, 1981.

Fast, I.: Gender Identity. A differentiation model. Adv. in Psychoanalysis, Theory Res and Practice. V. 2 Lawrence Assoc. Hillsdale, NJ 1984.

Freund, K.: Cross gender identity in a broader context. In: Gender Dysphoria. ed. B.W. Steiner, Plenum, New York, 1985, pp. 295-324.

Hoenig, J.: The origin of gender identity in gender dysphoria. (ed.) B.W. Steiner Plenum Press, New York, 1985, pp. 11-32.

Stoller, R.J.: Presentations of Gender. Yale Univ. Press, New Haven, 1985.

Storms, M.D.: A theory of erotic orientation development. Psychological Rev. 88: 340-353,1981.

Langevin, R.: Sexual Strands. Understanding and Treating Sexual Anamolies in Men. Lawrence Erlbaum Assoc. Hillsdale, NJ 1983.

Harry, J.: Sexual orientation as Destiny. J. Homosexuality. 10: 111-124, 1984.

Steiner, B.W.: Gender Dysphoria. Development Research Management. Plenum Press, New York,1985.

Levay S.: The Sexual Brain. Science, New Books, 1993.

Stress Mediated Effects on Sexual Identity

Hamburg, D.A. and Lunde, P.T.: Sex hormones in the development of sex differences in human behavior. In: The Development of Sex Differences (ed.) E.E. MacCory Stanford Univ. Press, Calif. 1966, pp 1-24.

Ward, I.L.: Prenatal stress feminizes and demasculinizes behavior of males. Sciences 175: 82-84, 1972.

Dahlof, L.G.; Hard, E. and Larsson, K.: Influence of maternal stress on offspring sexual behavior. Anim. Behav. 25: 958-963, 1977.

Whitney, J.B. and Herrenkohl, L.R.: Effect of anterior hypothalamic lesions on the sexual behavior of prenatally stressed male rat. Psych & Behav. 19: 167-169, 1977.

Ward, I.L. and Weisz, J.: Maternal stress alters plasma testosterone in fetal males. Science 207: 328-329, 1980.

Kalcheim, C.; Szechtman, H. and Koch, Y.: Bisexual behavior in male rats treated neonatally with antibodies to luteinizing hormone-releasing hormones. J. Comp. Physiol. Psychol. 95: 36-44, 1981.

Ehrhardt, A.A.; Meyer-Bahlurg, H.F.L.; Felzman. J.F. and Ince, S.E.: Sex-Dimorphic Behavior in childhood subsequent to prenatal exposure to exogenous progestogens and estrogens. Arch. Sex. Behav. 13: 457-477, 1984.

Ward, I.L.: The prenatal stress syndrome. Psychoneuroendocrin. 9: 3-11, 1984.

Central Nervous System

Grandy, K.L.; Phoenix, C.H. and Young, W.C: Role of the developing rat testis in differentiation of neural tissue mediating behavior. J. Comp. Physiol. Psychol. 59: 176-182, 1965.

Lehman, M.N.; Winans, S.S. and Powers, J.B.: Medial nucleus of the amygdala mediates chemosensory control of male hamster sexual behavior. Science 210: 557-560, 1980.

DeVoog, D.T. and Nottebohm, F.: Gonadal hormones induce dendritic growth in the adult avian brain. Science 214: 202-204, 1981.

Arnold, A.P. and Breedlove, S.M.: Organizational and activational effects of sex steroids on brain and behavior: A reanalysis. Hormones & Behavior. 19: 469-498, 1985.

Gennazzani, AR.; Gastaldi, M. Bidzinska, B.; Mercuri, N.; Genazzani, AD.; Nappi, RE.; Segre, A.; Petraglia, F.: The Brain as a Target Organ of Gonadal Steroids Psyconeuroendocrinol, 17: 385-390, 1992.

Alzheimer's and Parkinson's Disease: Smell Deficiency

McCaffery, R.J.; Duff, K. and Solomon, S.G.: Olfactory dysfunction discrimnate probable Alzheimer's dementia from major depression: A cross validation and extension. J. Neuropsychiatry Clin. Neurosci. 12: 29-33, 2000.

Liberni, P.; Parola, S.; Sprano, P.F. and Antonini,L.: Olfaction in Parkinson's Disease: A methods of assessment and clinical relevance. J. Neurol. 247: 88-96, 2000.

Kareken, D.A.; Doty, R.L.; Moberg, P.J. et al.: Olfactory evoked regional cerebral blood flow in Alzheimer's disease. Neuropsychology 15: 18-29, 2000.

Histocompatability and Odor: A clue to odor compatability.

Yamazaki, K.; Boyse,E.A.; Mike, V.: Thaler, H.T.; Mathieson, B.J.; Abbott,J.; Boyse, J.; Zayas, Z.A. and Thomas, L.: Control of mating preferences in mice by genes in the major histocompatabilty complex. J.Exp. Med. 144: 1324-1335, 1976.

Yamazaki, K.; Yamaguchi, M; Baronoski, K.; Bard, J.; Boyse, E.A.; Thomas, L.: Recognition among mice: Evidence from the use of a Y-maze differentially scented by congenic mice of different major histocompatability types. J. Exp. Med. 150: 755-760, 1979.

Jones, J.S. and Partridge, L.: Tissue rejection: The price of sexual acceptance? Nature 304: 484-485, 1983.

Boyse, J.; Beauchamp,G.K.; Yamazaki,K.; Bard, J. and Thomas, L.: A new aspect of the major histocompatability complex and other genes in the mouse. Oncodevelopmental Biol. & Med. 4: 101-116, 1982.

Tantric Buddhism

Shaw, M. " Everything You Always Wanted to Know About Tantra," An Interview with Craig Hamilton. Enlightenment 13: 36-47, 1998.

Shaw, M. Passionate Enlightenment. Princeton, 1994.

Index